Dodging the 60's Bullet:

And Other Blessings from My Mennonite German Immigrant Grandparents

by Barbara Wyman

DORRANCE PUBLISHING CO
EST. 1920
PITTSBURGH, PENNSYLVANIA 15238

Dorrance Publishing Co
585 Alpha Drive
Pittsburgh, PA 15238
Visit our website at *www.dorrancebookstore.com*

ISBN: 979-8-88925-358-7
eISBN: 979-8-88925-858-2

Chapter 1
IT BEGINS

I was around 19 years old, heading toward the front door on my way to catch the bus to work when I heard my grandfather call my name. I answered, "What, Grandpa?" He was seated, as usual, in his chair in the corner of the living room listening to the radio.

With his Bible in his lap, he sounded upset, declaring, "I'm afraid folks are beginning to confuse liberty with license!" I probably muttered something polite and left for my salesclerk job at the local JC Penney's store.

It was almost 1963, and I had graduated from high school in 1961. I don't remember thinking too much about what my 88-year-old grandfather had said that morning, but I did notice some signs of a shift in social norms following that school year. Signs like dress codes that suddenly allowed girls to wear pants, boys to wear jeans… and even more shocking, *tennis shoes*, even if you were not in sports!

My high school had over 3000 students for grades tenth through twelfth. In the years I attended, there were no major social issues that I knew of. Teen pregnancies were unknown (or hidden), but some girls were rumored to be 'easy' or 'cheap' depending on their reputations. Most offences were for chewing gum or talking during class time. Respect was expected, and parents trusted teachers to discipline if needed. Missing school was unacceptable and rare, except for a serious illness or injury, and in my family, skipping school would have been considered a mortal sin! We said the Pledge of Allegiance with our hands over our hearts every day, but prayer was never part of the school day at that time. There was some bullying then, but not on the scale it happens now.

The next few years seemed generally the same culturally, but by the later '60s, I was amazed to learn that if you had a baby while in high school you could have the baby included in your annual picture! Some schools were even providing childcare on the premises. Pot smoking was also starting to be an okay thing to do as well. Back then I thought that smoking pot was just something done by 'beatniks' that wore all black and hung out in underground jazz clubs in New York City where poetry reading was also part of the entertainment. During that time, I began to see the results of these changes when my younger cousin started college. She, along with most, got into the whole pot-smoking, anything-goes culture that eventually exploded with the 1969 Wood-stock celebration of casual sex, drugs, and hard rock. Before then the assassination of President Kennedy in 1963, his brother Robert and Martin Luther king shocked our senses. In addition, the war in Vietnam had contrib-uted to a rebellion by this generation against the government and our Armed Forces as well. Four college students were even shot dead during an anti-war protest at Kent State University by the military. A lot was changing rapidly, and from what I observed, not for the best.

On reflection, I realize that my grandfather was simply seeing a disturbing trend and wanted me to see it as he did. He was a kind and wise man who never preached but lived by his Christian faith and values.

By sheer luck (or God's plan), I was born just a little too soon to get a direct hit by what I am calling the '60s bullet. And I now realize I was further blessed by belonging to this unique family of German Mennonite immigrants!

Choosing America:

On March 10, 1882, my grandfather and his family arrived at Ellis Island. He was about 12 years old and a member of the Mennonite church. They left Germany to seek religious freedom in America because of the mandated mil-itary service that was against their Mennonite creed. (There is no biblical scrip-ture that supports this belief, but I will leave that to a later chapter). At that time, there was no 'safety net' for immigrants. They were required to prove they were healthy, able to support themselves, even while having a sponsor. In addition, they were expected to have employable skills and the ability to speak, or the commitment to learn, English.

The Mennonite church culture is much like the Amish in that they hold to a strict code of behavior and outward appearance. Their basic beliefs are Christian, honoring the Ten Commandments and living a life of honesty, jus-tice, and sexual morality. But eventually some additional expectations became too restrictive for my grandparents. They decided to leave the church not long after they moved to Seattle in 1916 from Oklahoma with their seven children when my dad was six weeks old. One of the church issues was my grand-mother's hair. Mennonite women were not allowed to cut their hair and had to wear it in a bun. My grandmother had very thick chestnut brown hair, and when she put it in a bun, some of it tended to fall forward around her forehead. My grandfather was told by the church that his wife needed to be 'less worldly' in how she appeared. Another problem occurred because my grandfather worked as an expert tailor in an exclusive downtown store. He was soon told by the church that he was not to do any tailoring for women as that would require him to do arm or other body measurements that were considered immoral contact with a female other than his wife.

My grandparents never left their Christian faith, just the church. Even without a church, they raised their children with all the best of their faith, and this was another blessing that prevented the '60s bullet from mortally wounding me!

They married in 1900 in Peoria, Illinois. My grandmother was a nurse, but my grandfather wanted to be a farmer and for some reason they opted to move to Cherokee, Oklahoma! For several years they made a heroic effort to have a farm and raise children. (I recall my grandfather once asking me to never serve parsnips because it was almost all they could grow during those constant drought years). If you are wondering what parsnips are like…they are a root vegetable like a carrot, only whitish and more like a horse radish in texture. They have a somewhat spicy-bitter taste and not good to eat raw. I imagine they ate them boiled, baked, mashed, and fried. (I actually don't mind them in a stew or mashed with some butter and sour crème…however they are not on my current grocery list of have-to-haves.)

My grandmother gave birth to 8 children…2 girls and 6 boys. There were two sets of twins (one set of boys and the other a boy and girl). Sadly, the baby girl died at just 6 weeks. After years of the ongoing drought, life there was much harder than *Little House on the Prairie*, so they finally gave up and moved to Seattle where they hoped to begin a better life.

With help from relatives they purchased acreage just north of the Seattle city limits and built their own two-story home with a basement, 3 bedrooms and one bath.

My grandfather fulfilled some of his farming dreams by planting a massive number of fruit trees and gardens with every berry known to man as well as every vegetable possible (except parsnips). He added a large chicken coop, grew red and green grapes, and made his own wine, which he hardly ever drank.

The basement was full of wine barrels and canned fruits and vegetables. Along with all the growing, harvesting and canning I also watched my grandmother when she killed and de-feathered a chicken for dinner. Her style was to wring their necks by holding their feet and swinging them in a circle over her head, while my grandfather used the quicker head chop-off method. His style resulted in the chicken running around without its head for a few minutes… gross! (Hence the old adage 'Running around like a chicken with its head cut off!', sometimes used to describe how some people act under stress.)

My family lived in a small house next door and I spent lots of time at their house. When I was about 5 years old grandma asked me to get some eggs from the chicken coop. I said I was scared they might peck me, but she told me it would be okay if I just gently pushed them aside and take all but one egg from each nest. She was right, and I proudly brought her the basket of fresh eggs without getting pecked! Looking back my grandmother had to be the original Martha Stewart of that time! She harvested and canned everything that grew with the 'waste-not-want-not' mentality from going through the Great Depression, as well as her Mennonite and Oklahoma experience. She was a great cook who also knew how to add ambiance to each meal! (Who else serves a sectioned grapefruit with powdered sugar and a maraschino cherry on top for breakfast…for grade school kids?) She also did the laundry without an automatic washer and drier and made her own soap with bacon fat she saved on the stove.

After each day's work she would sit by her husband and continue making the beautiful quilts she designed with tiny fabric scraps she kept in a basket. My grandfather read aloud to her from the Bible until time to go to bed. Sometimes she repaired holes in the socks she kept in another basket. She rarely spoke but taught me how to do this as well. I learned to use a 'darning needle' to carefully weave threads back and forth over the hole that was stretched across what I can only describe as a plastic egg attached to a stick. I cannot imagine teaching a child in today's world how, or why, this was done; along with so many other chores that were part of normal housekeeping then. To this day I marvel at how my grandmother perfectly fit the profile of the 'godly' woman described in Christian scripture…her hands were never idle!

I did not even know we were German until I was an adult! They spoke and wrote perfect English and my grandfather did not allow German to be used in their home. He wanted to be an American, and his greatest hero was Abraham Lincoln. He had a friend who brought him a large poster depicting Lincoln pardoning a soldier who had gone AWOL to see his ill mother. Lincoln deeply loved his own mother and granted the pardon. The title on the poster says "JUSTICE TO ALL". In the background of the portrait there are two horses being tended to by soldiers. The friend told my grandfather that he knew a man who knew the soldier tending Lincoln's horse. Knowing how fond of Lincoln my grandfather was, he thought the poster would be appreciated as a gift. Well, it was eventually framed and hung in the dining room for as long as I can remember. It is dated 1921 and was willed to me after I begged my grandfather for it. It hangs in my living room now and has been willed to Sasha at her request!

In addition to their pride in America I also feel blessed to have grandparents who never even spoke harshly to each other; or to anyone else for that matter. But I do remember my grandfather's story of how he once threatened a man who was whipping a horse! He said he told him he would do the same to the man if he ever saw him doing it again! My grandfather was a kind and gentle man, but he could be very firm and we never doubted that we were expected to behave; and that included treating animals with kindness.

You may be wondering by now how I remember all this about them. Well, we continued living next door until my mother left when I was about 7 years old, and often spent time with them. Later on our circumstances changed and my dad eventually decided to rent out our house to help with income. I think I was about 8 years old when we moved in with my grandparents and this was the home I lived in until I married at age 20.

My grandfather's beloved poster of
Abraham Lincoln

Marie with my dad 1916

March 4, 1900 Peoria, IL. Mennonite
weddings portrait of my German
grandparents, Marie and Frederick

My grandparents after a trip back east
(coats made by him!)

A family portrait with my dad on
grandpa's lap. (all clothing made by
him. Except the shirts and dresses).
About 1921.

Marie's nursing portrait

Their 6 sons and one daughter
(my dad center bottom row)

Chapter 2
THE NEXT 'BLESSING'?

'Out on the town' 1946- My mother 4th from the right, my dad 2nd from the right

I had two brothers; one was almost 4 and one was 10, when our mother decided to leave. The day she left she came outside where the three of us were playing in the yard to tell us she was going downtown to get thread and would be home later.

My dad got home from his city bus-driving job around 5 p.m. and asked us where our mother was. We told him what she said, and we all went inside. He straightened up the house and started to fix us some dinner when she was still not home. He called the Diner where she had recently started a part time job, as well as all their friends and relatives to see if they knew where she was. I did not know until much later how distressed he was as we were soon put in different homes so he could begin searching for her as a missing person with the police, trying to identify the bodies of dead women. This went on for a few weeks. We found out later that during this time, my mother's mother knew where she was and would not tell my dad, even though my older brother was temporarily placed in her home!

I was placed with my dad's best friend and his wife. They had a 10-year-old daughter and only a crib for me to sleep in. I was 7 and very upset about this humiliation! My younger brother was with a family I can't recall, but my dad took us to visit him as much as possible. I remember watching out the back window of our old Oldsmobile as we drove away after leaving him with a new teddy bear. He was holding it tight, looking out the widow until we were out of sight. Later on, I found out that one of my uncles wanted to adopt me, and others offered to keep my brothers. My dad said 'NO' to everyone and got us back with him as soon as he found our mothers' goodbye note in the drawer of her sewing machine. (The thread connection?) He told us the note said she hated him and hated everything in general, I guess. I never did read it for myself.

One of my mother's fashion designs

We soon were back in our home with dad. My younger brother was looked after next door by my grandmother while our dad worked and my older brother and I went to school. My dad did everything he could to keep house for us, doing almost as much as before she left. He loved her and let her do as she pleased which was spending most of each day doing watercolors of clothing designs instead of housework and cooking. She was a talented artist and designer and could have made a career in that field if she had pursued it. I remember the neighbors coming over after they were done with their housework to sit around watching her paint. They were still having coffee; smoking and chatting when we came home from school. My dad would come home after work and do laundry and help with other chores. My mother loved being out 'on the town', but our working-class income was not very suited to that. My dad also liked music and dancing and would take her out as often as possible. I never heard him raise his voice to her and there was no abuse of any kind that I can recall. He also did not object when she wanted to take a part time job at that local Diner.

I eventually found out that my mother had first gone to California with a guy she had met at the Diner; and had expected my dad to come looking for her! When this did not happen, she went to New York and took a job at a hotel in Manhattan. Apparently she wrote my dad telling him she was 'devastated' that he never came looking for her; and asked him to send her clothes. He wrote her back telling her she would have to come and get them herself. Shortly after that she married an alcoholic chef who worked at the same hotel and soon gave birth to 4 more children.

This seemed a little odd as we thought she didn't like being a mother! Later, I heard from family and friends that her idea of taking care of kids was just to let them basically raise themselves. She once left my younger brother in his crib so long that he had scooped out his diaper and decorated as much of his crib and walls with the warm brown stuff as he could! I was also told that my grandfather would often see my brother outside in a playpen for hours and would go sit next to him on the ground to keep him company.

Despite all this, by the time I was in 6th grade I attempted to 'forgive' her. I did not know she had remarried, and I thought that since she was divorced and in New York she was free to start a job with a clothing company, or a designer where she could build a career using her talent; but that was apparently not in her. It was the mid-'50s and many women were trying to 'find themselves', rebelling against being just a housewife and mother. I wrote her a few letters that she answered until my dad found out. It made him so upset I asked her to stop, which she did. Later on my brothers and I asked him why he didn't find us a new mom. He calmly explained that he could not trust that another woman would care as much about us as he did.

In looking back, I believe the stress and exhaustion he endured eventually took its toll years later when my dad collapsed at the wheel of his bus in downtown Seattle. Fortunately, the bus rolled into a curb in front of a building and there were no injuries. This made the front page of the *Seattle Times*, minus the probable cause.

Single Parenting:

Now that I am in my sunset years, I cannot believe what a remarkable father we were blessed with. It is heart-breaking to hear about the many children that are harmed by a parent who puts their own desire for a partner ahead of their children. (This I know personally for a later chapter I might title *Thank God for Forgiveness*.)

My dad took all three of us to every new Disney movie, every annual 'Ice Capades', roller skating, bowling and always the Puyallup fair each year! We went camping and on road trips to Mount Rainier and the Woodland Park Zoo. He got my brothers into scouting, sports, and music lessons. I failed miserably at piano, and he agreed with the instructor that I was hopeless after a year of it. (I was an okay singer though!). My older brother got pretty good on the guitar and my younger one wasn't too bad on the trumpet. One thing we all missed were the family get-togethers on my mothers' side! Her family was full of professional jazz musicians and every time we visited them it was a jam session! My dad even played a Hawaiian steel guitar fairly well and taught me how to ballroom dance. In my teens I also became his 'dance partner' on several occasions, like the annual Bowling Banquet, or a wedding reception!

When I was about 10, our grandmother passed away at age 80 and he decided to hire a housekeeper. This decision included her teenage daughter! We tried to call the housekeeper 'mom', but she firmly said to call her Aunt Mildred. She shared a bedroom with her daughter while my dad and grandfather shared the larger main bedroom, and I had the smallest 3rd bedroom. My two brothers shared a room in the basement that had been used as my grandfathers' tailor shop. Sometime later, one of my uncles and his daughter moved in after his divorce. I then had to share my small room with my younger cousin, and her dad slept in a twin bed in the corner of the main bedroom. Nine of us…and one small bathroom! It had a sink, toilet, and tub without a shower. We were only allowed to bathe once a week and I washed my hair in the kitchen sink.

Eventually Aunt Mildred and her daughter decided to return to Louisiana after they had saved enough money to do so. I was about 12 years old then and remember sitting at the kitchen table with my dad and brothers when he confided to us that he did not think he could afford another housekeeper. Being my ignorant, almost-in-junior-high-pre-teen self; I proudly declared that I could do everything Aunt Mildred did! My dad just stared at me for a bit, then told me to try doing it if I really wanted to.

Well, it must be that God gives young people an amazing amount of energy, because I cannot believe how much I was doing during those years. I know for a fact that my family suffered through some lame meals until I improved by trial and error. Every night my dad would wash the dishes and sing while I dried and put them away. This is when I learned all the '40s songs I still remember to this day. We would talk about lots of things, but one time I saw just how irritated he could get. We were chatting as usual, and I piped up with my arrogant teenage opinion that having kids was not something I wanted to do. He sharply informed me that only the most self-centered people refused to have children. Well, I know some very nice people who made that choice; but will never forget how strongly he reacted to my statement!

My dad had sacrificed so much for us, and after becoming a parent myself, I wish I had told him how much I loved him. (Being of traditional German heritage, expressions of affection were not easily shared in our family.)

When he passed away, we bought a beautiful marble box for his ashes and buried it alongside his parents' gravesite with only a few others attending. We each had a red rose to place on the box, and before it was covered with earth, I decided to sing one of his favorite songs: "It's a Sin to Tell a Lie":

"Be sure it's true when you say: I love you, it's a sin to tell a lie. Millions of hearts have been broken just because these little words were spoken. I love you, yes, I do, I love you. If you break my heart, I'll die. So be sure that it's true when you say, 'I love you'; it's a sin to tell a lie."

I love you, Dad…we were blessed to be raised by you.

1953, my single dad with me and my younger brother on a visit to the Smith Tower in Seattle

My mother and dad between her brother and sister

1956, my dad with my younger brother

1946, family picnic (Grandpa always well-dressed)

Dad & me 1943

My mother and dad 'horsing around' with a friend (on the right)

My dad in his uniform by our Oldsmobile (probably in the 40s)

My dad and mother before she left in
1950

1950 with my younger brother- the
year our mother left

Me and my older brother 1945

Around 1942, my mother with her
mother and my older brother

my younger brother- 1949

Before 1950 in our backyard

1946 at a family picnic

1943 when I was born

My family in 1948

Chapter 3
PRE- '60s SCHOOL STUFF, ETC.

As mentioned earlier, I want to relate some experiences to show that the pre-'60s era was not completely exempt from many of the social problems that are even more amplified today.

Sadly, some of my own teenage choices were less than admirable. Even though my family did not attend church, I was raised with the Christian doctrine known as the 'Golden Rule': that we should always treat others as we wished to be treated. Despite this I still decided to be part of a little gang of 'mean girls' at my junior high. There were three of them, all from the families of wealthy doctors who lived in the 'better' neighborhoods. Oddly, there was a fourth 'tag-along' girl, Sally, who they made fun of and verbally tormented continually. (Thank God there was no social media then to make it worse!) I did not treat this girl badly, but I also wanted to be accepted by these bullies for some, still unknown, reason.

Every Saturday, after my chores, we would meet up in downtown Seattle to do our favorite activity of shop-lifting makeup and nail polish from the 'Five and Dime' stores. There were two of these big stores that also had lunch counters where you could get an egg salad or Tuna sandwich with at least three potato chips and a soft drink for $1.25! But whenever Sally was on the other side of the store, the three would start yelling at her, calling her 'Pizza Face' because of her acne, and other names to embarrass her. (Oddly, even though Sally always wanted to be part of our weekend jaunts, I don't recall her ever stealing anything!) Back at school, the three would continue to torment her and be as obnoxious as they could to anyone else they chose to make miserable. I just went along as best I could until something happened that changed everything.

We were all in the same home economics class one day when the teacher was trying to explain how to boil eggs or something. I heard the three starting in on Sally who had her head down on her desk, quietly sobbing. As usual the teacher just ignored the whole spectacle when something inside me snapped. I raised my hand and asked for permission to take the sobbing girl to the restroom. The teacher (I think gladly) allowed me to do that. I then went over to Sally and touched her on the arm asking her to come with me. When we got into the restroom, she was still quietly sobbing. I told her that from now on I would be her friend and we did not need the other three to be part of our lives anymore. She finally stopped crying and we went back to class.

The amazing thing was how quickly it all *stopped!* Not the three bullies, they stayed that way, but they never bothered us after that! Why did this happen? Why did I suddenly want to protect this girl and leave the 'gang'? Did I need this wake-up call? All I know is a different path was presented to me, and I also soon learned that Sally was a born-again Christian.

This timid girl eventually asked me to come to a Youth-For-Christ meeting after school with her. This was where I first heard the story of the crucifixion of Jesus, his resurrection and purpose. I remember feeling overwhelmed with sorrow and the need to be 'saved'. I raised my hand that day and asked Christ to forgive and accept me. (These after-school 'religious clubs' were not scorned or threatened like they are now.) After attending YFC a few more times, I started going to church with Sally. It was a large Presbyterian church about a mile from our neighborhoods. I never became a member but took part in youth group and sang in the choir. We also performed duets frequently during services. She had a piano at her house, and we also had one; so we took turns practicing and visiting at each other's homes as often as possible. Sally would play the piano and sing soprano while I was the alto harmony. I had to subdue my voice because hers was at a much softer volume. I know my grandfather really loved hearing us practice next to where he sat every night. (He had been a long-time member of the men's choir before leaving the Mennonite church and I still have some of the German hymnals he had used.)

A 'Christian' Home-life:

During my friendship with Sally, I was soon to discover another reality: that not all who claim to be Christians live a 'Christ-like' life. The first time I went to her home after school, I was surprised at how dark the house was. All the blinds were down, and her mom was in the kitchen with a baby in a kind of sling on her back. Sally's dad was in an overstuffed chair in the living room just staring straight ahead. After school one day, when Sally asked her mom about something, she grabbed Sally's purse, swung it over her head and hit her with it! Sally just started softly sobbing, and we went upstairs to her room. The upstairs was just an attic, but we would sit on her bed talking and then go through her clothes to see what she could share for me to wear. We would do the same when she visited at my house because we were both too poor for each of us to have much of a wardrobe.

Most of the time at her house was spent practicing our duets for church, but we would also sometimes leave to walk to the library or a drugstore before it got dark. One time as we were leaving, her dad called her over to yell at her for being "made-up like a prostitute" because she had used mascara. Another time in the early evening, I heard her dad firmly let her mom know that he was ready for bed, and she dutifully followed him. (I don't have any memory of either of them smiling or laughing.)

I had not experienced this kind of a family and wondered how this very sweet Christian girl had turned out like she was. She also had an older brother, a real 'rebel' who would sit next to their dad with a six-pack of beer, drinking and blowing cigar smoke in his face! For some reason, their dad just seemed to tolerate it. Her brother left home right after high school. A few years later, Sally's dad suffered a stroke or something and was eventually in a wheelchair.

We never talked much about our families, but Sally had to have noticed the differences. My home was bright and welcoming. There was no name calling or berating of anyone I can recall. (And there was a lot of smiling and laughing!)

Our home was not perfect; my dad was a chain smoker and grandpa chewed tobacco. One of my chores was to clean his spittoon on Saturdays, which I really did not mind because he was always so appreciative. Despite these things, the house was always a pleasant place to be. In Sally's house, there was no décor on the walls like we had. Our walls had beautifully framed mirrors as well as some paintings with candle sconces alongside. My grandmother had good taste in furnishings, and she even had small plants and various objects lining the window sills in the breakfast nook. Many of these items were gifts from one of her sons during his military service that he sent from the countries he was stationed in. There were several large plants in the living room that I became the caregiver of. One was about four feet tall with huge thick leaves that my grandmother insisted be wiped clean every week with milk! We also had a pet parakeet that could recite part of "Peter Peter, Pumpkin Eater" and at least one cat or two that added to the family mix. Sally's home had no pets or plants.

I don't recall what kind of church her parents were part of, just that they did not attend the one we went to. I have since realized that there is a lot of misunderstanding regarding the teachings of Christ. Even though my family did not attend a church, they were happy that I did! This was strange because my own father was an agnostic. I often pray that he was still welcomed in Heaven as only God knows the human heart. (There was much about my father that might surprise some, but I am saving that for another chapter.)

Holidays were always celebrated in our home with some home-made decorations. At Thanksgiving I would beg my older brother to make his fabulous cornucopia out of aluminum foil. He *hated* doing this as much as he hated when I would beg him to make the Christmas decorations. He would eventually do it, and I would fill this Thanksgiving 'masterpiece' with fake and real fruits and vegetables for the holiday table. It looked quite beautiful, and my grandmother would have me polish the good silverware, get out the crystal flutes for shrimp cocktails as well as the delicate wine glasses. After we set the table covered with her best lace cloth, my grandfather would say grace and the feast would be as spectacular as it was every year!

Christmas proved even more of a pain for my brother. I would get a wire coat hanger every December and bend it into a circle. As soon as he saw me with it, he would loudly protest: "NO, NO and *NO!*" It was futile, of course, as I pointed him to the large fir and holly tree in our yard and reminded him to get enough of the boughs to do the top of the piano (with lights), and enough to wind along the stairway where the stockings would be hung. Before too long, he would finish these creations that would be the envy of anyone who saw them. I told him it was not my fault that he was such an artist, but only got a scowl back from him!

Me with my two brothers 1958   Me 1952   Me 1953

Chapter 4
HIGH SCHOOL HIERARCHY and '50s LIFE

Some things never change, such as our human nature to divide into groups, but this is something that cannot be blamed on the "60s Bullet'. I'm pretty sure anyone reading this knows what I'm referring to when it comes to experiencing this in high school, or even earlier, regardless of your generation.

We all have seen this to be true with culture, religion, occupations, income, physical appearance, etc. Some might even sum it all up with 'birds of a feather flock together'. This is never more obvious than in an average high school like Sally and I went to; just the 'flock' names have changed with each generation.

My older Brother and the car he kept me out of

In my school there were the following groups: One of them was the *soc* click (pronounced like the first syllable of social). These were kids from wealthy families that always wore the latest and most expensive clothes and shoes. They were the cool and popular kids. If you were a female *soc*, you were usually pretty, wore cashmere or angora sweaters, the popular white 'Bucks' shoes from Nordstrom's and matching socks. Everyone knew that the non-*soc* girls could only afford the imitation white 'Bucks' from a store called Leeds, and sweaters from JC Penney's or even K-Mart (talking Seattle here). A *soc* would rarely be seen associating with a non-*soc*. A male *soc* was usually also a '*jock*'. Any athlete, especially a Letterman, was part of this group. And only a *soc* could be on the cheerleading squads. These teens were often given special privileges and more positive attention from teachers as well. It was rumored that this group also partied it up with beer and other adult beverages in their homes when the parents were out. (Quite shocking at that time!) Despite their wealthy status in the pre-'60s, only a few had cars! Oddly enough, many in another group called the *greasers* did!

My older brother was in this category. The *greasers* hung out in front of a small store across from the school, wore black leather jackets, had greased hair, and smoked cigarettes. They tried to look like Elvis or James Dean with an attitude. (Think John Travolta in *Grease*). Some had hot-rod cars for drag racing and impressing girls. My brother pretended to be one of them, but he always got out of any dicey situations with his humor. He would joke about himself as "I'm so skinny I could take a shower inside a garden hose!" He never got into any real trouble, and actually became an Eagle Scout later! In his senior year, he was able to save enough from a paper route and other small jobs to buy our dad's old, dark green Oldsmobile. He had it painted a deep metallic red with white pin stripes. He glued a fake fur piece to the dashboard and hung the head of a dried baby alligator from the visor. (It was too cool.) He added white-wall tires; always kept it perfect and wouldn't let me near it.

A third group was the *nerds*. These were the bookworms, the science and math-smart kids, mostly non-athletic boys, but a few girls as well. They kept to themselves and didn't ask for attention. They took a lot of teasing and scorn from the *soc* and *greaser* crowds, but they often wound up having better lives after high school than most of the 'cool' kids.

Sally and I fell into a group that had no name. We were none of the above. We were with the 'nobody' kids who could not afford the clothes or the White Buck shoes from Nordstrom's, and we were lucky to earn a C average and graduate. As a senior, I joined up with the students that liked to perform in plays and talent shows. There were even a few *soc* kids that took part, but most of them saw it as a joke to do for an elective (not required) class. I remember being the only one in the plays that knew everyone's lines! When they had that blank look, forgetting their lines, I would whisper it to them from the sidelines. (Good grief.) But I did get straight A's in drama and won 'Best Supporting Actress' at the Drama Festival!

Dealing With It:

There were two things that helped me deal with these social issues during school and beyond: my dad's lectures and my Christianity. Being the daughter of a female most of my family called a 'Clothes-Horse', I felt shamed for wanting to dress better or follow the current fads like the *soc* girls. Whenever I would whine about this to my dad, I would get 'the talk'. He would sit next to me on my bed and patiently explain that if I or my brothers wore clothes that were neat and clean, and acted respectably, we would be welcome anywhere. He said if I wanted anything more than he could provide, I should earn the money myself but added I should never feel that having more clothes or following the fads would make me a better or happier person.

Okay… thanks, Dad. Well, reluctantly, I had to admit that Jesus agreed with my dad. Just quickly skimming through the words of Christ should convince anyone that God will never judge us on our wardrobes (unless it consists of robes trimmed with numerous long tassels while we are out preaching on the streets. See Matthew 23:5). In addition, Jesus told us not to fret about what to wear, etc. and to notice the birds and flowers that are more beautiful than any man-made creation. Even so there *are* some passages where people are admonished for not being dressed appropriately, like for a wedding, or other important ceremonies, but this was a matter of showing respect. I am pretty sure Christ never meant it was okay to look like an unkempt slob! Try a trip to a Wal-Mart or sit in a courtroom today and see how many have no clue regarding respect. (Not sure if this can be blamed on the '60s bullet either, but a lot of the counter-culture, anti-conservative, who-cares attitudes did get started around then.)

One incident with me and Sally about how we chose to dress is a real glimpse into what has changed since the '50s.

We were about 15 years old and decided to walk up the hill to the corner store. We were wearing our baggy, knee-length Bermuda shorts with our baggy sweatshirts, our clunky 'saddle' shoes, and ankle high socks.

Our walk took us past my aunt's house where she was looking out her window. She called us in. Well, you'd think we were wearing tank tops and Daisy Dukes with fishnet stockings and six-inch heels (you know, like a typical 11-year-old girl at school today!). Anyway, we got a scolding that would make a professional hooker cry! She asked us if we were aware of just how dangerous it was to be out dressed like that, and did we not realize that any pervert driving around would not hesitate to kidnap and do 'God-knows-what' terrible things to us? Well, obviously we were clueless, but I can't remember if we changed clothes or just went home that day. (I can imagine if you are reading this and are not over 50, you might be in shock that anyone would consider our outfits to be provocative at all.)

This is only one example of what was different before the era of my grandfather's perception that liberty was starting to be confused with license.

Sex sells:

This brings me to the first time I heard the 'S' word on TV and radio. It was about 1962 when I overheard an ad for toothpaste as I was heading out one day. A musical voice-over was touting the virtues of this item calling it the "toothpaste with sex appeal". I was shocked! This word had *never* been used to sell anything! Little did I know how much was about to change and, in my opinion, not for the better.

Even Hollywood in the pre-'60s was pretty tame when it came to love scenes as well as profanity. These films almost never showed blatant nudity or intimate sexual scenes, leaving all that to the viewer's imagination. You never had to be embarrassed when on a first date or had your grandmother or young children watching. They offered a story without the explicit scenes that are now a normal part of most movies today. What is perplexing to me is the fact that Hollywood does not seem to care that a good story without gratuitous sex scenes out-sells the rest every time! Perhaps money is not the only goal?

This is another part of the social decline that began in the '60s when sexuality stopped being looked at as a gift created by a loving God. This 'gift' was specifically designed for a man and a woman to become 'one' with each other, but only in marriage. According to God's word in scripture, it describes sexual intimacy outside of marriage as sinful because we would then 'become one flesh', even if it is with a prostitute (1st Corinthians, 6:13-20).

When sex became just another way to sell stuff, be entertained with, or for momentary gratification, the proverbial 'Pandora's box' was opened.

Chapter 5
TURN ON, TUNE IN and DROP OUT

Early in the '60s, a popular professor named Timothy Leary introduced the idea that a powerful psychedelic drug called LSD would be a 'cure-all' for everything he believed was wrong in the world. He was only one of the many left-leaning (now called progressive) teachers hired by colleges throughout the country. During this time, God was also being declared dead, and almost every traditional value was being challenged or dismissed as oppressive. These 'elite' folks were also promoting the New-Age concept that Christian beliefs were retarding mankind's true spiritual evolvement.

Soon many of Leary's students took him up on his ideas; so, LSD and other 'hard drugs' were added to the scene along with the common pot and alcohol use that were part of college life.

It is interesting that Bible scripture speaks of this issue in a section warning against occult practices. In Galatians 5:19-21, Revelation 18: 23, 21:8 and other scriptures, the Greek word 'pharmakeia' was translated as 'sorceries' and used in a list of things that God forbids. Pagan worshipers often used various mind-altering substances to enhance their experiences and attempts to contact the spirit world. Our word for drugs (pharmaceuticals) is derived from the Greek 'pharmakeia', and this word was also used along with 'the schemes of Satan' in some Christian writings. The Greek dictionary also defines 'pharmakeia' as witchcraft, or magic spells and potions.

Mind-altering experiences have always been popular. I remember as a child spinning around as fast as I could outside until I collapsed on the ground feeling the rush of dizziness overtake me. Many seek the experience of bungee-jumping and other high-risk activities because of the adrenalin 'rush'. Even Mid-eastern style Yoga meditation can induce an altered state of mind. (I am not alone in believing this practice can also invite spirits that may not have one's best interest at heart.)

Not all these things are as harmful to the human psyche as some of these mind-bending drugs are. In addition to the desire to escape reality for a time, I believe the main reason is to subdue the inhibitions that usually stop us from doing stupid, harmful, and immoral things. There are now some of the deadliest drugs on our streets that no one thought would ever be created. Witness the daily reports of child abuse, murders and personal destruction from meth. Another drug called 'bath salts' can cause someone to actually attack a person for no reason and try to bite off their face! Then there is fentanyl, a drug so powerful that a taser will not stop an attacker. And, of course, we still have heroin with the jump to that from opiate use. All of this is adding to the current rise in homelessness and crime as well.

Growing up in the '50s, drinking socially as adults was acceptable, but alcoholism was not, and drug use was not even in the picture except for a medical need. In my family, my dad would have an occasional beer, and on a special occasion with friends might have what he called 'schnapps' (usually a shot of whisky). I remember he allowed us a taste of beer once but made it absolutely clear that alcohol was something *only* an adult could drink, and only in moderation. We were never to forget that his choice to have a drink in no way gave us permission to do the same. He said as long as he was our provider, and we were not 21, it was not okay. We were continually taught that some things were only for adults. I have had many people tell me that if your kids see you drinking you have given them permission to do it too. (I think these are the same people that believe they should be their children's friend instead of a parent.) I used to ask them if this logic was applied shouldn't their underage kids be able to drive the family car? How about watching an X-rated movie? These questions would usually just get a blank stare for a response.

Obviously, children living with alcoholics or drug addicts are not being nurtured and monitored in a stable home, so it would be logical that they would feel free to experiment, and many do become addicts as well. Along with that is the truth that a young, developing brain can be altered permanently. I also have a bit of an issue with those who claim that drugs are no worse than alcohol. I have yet to see the evidence for this considering the kind of brain damage some of these drugs can cause. In addition to this is the time it takes to become an alcoholic compared to the almost instant addiction and damage with the worst of these drugs.

The drug legacy of the '60s remains one of the most destructive of that era we are seeing today. It has infected every part of life, including the belief that even prescribed drugs are the answer to every problem. When childhood behavior was diagnosed as ADHD or ADD (Attention Deficit Disorder), a drug was given to calm or focus the child. Too many parents allowed these drugs to be given at the slightest suggestion from a teacher or counselor, and there has been no research, that I know of, as to the long-term effects of these drugs. The privacy laws that prevent us from knowing just how these drugs affect a criminal action are almost demonic as far as I'm concerned. When a child is on these drugs starting at age 3 and then at 16 shoots up a school, are we ever told the possible connection?

Another negative aspect of the prevalent use of mind-altering substances is how they are used to justify bad behavior. My own experience of this was during my unfortunate, but brief, second marriage. My husband was abusive (drunk or sober actually), and I was volunteering at a counseling service when I told the staff about his behavior. I explained that he would usually apologize and claim it was just because he was drinking. The lead psychologist then told me that people don't abuse because they drink; they drink so they can abuse. After many years of observation, I have become convinced of the truth in that psychologist's statement. I am also convinced that the lack of a moral compass is the perfect breeding ground for the abuse of drugs and alcohol, and this is further compounded by the excuse they provide for immoral or criminal acts.

I am writing about this on October 18, 2020, and just this morning read an article on Fox News that perfectly illustrates this drug excuse problem. According to the article, the molestation of a 7-year-old girl was caught live (on screen) in the home of the girl while she was attending an on-line class due to the COVID-19 lockdown requirement. These online classes are such that they are interactive, meaning the student can see the class and they can see the student and the room they are in. The teacher and other students saw what was happening and contacted police. The police arrested the suspect, Catrell Walls, an 18-year-old male cousin of the victim. The attorney for the defense is claiming that the suspect suffers from 'impulse control' due to being ADHD. (He has been on drugs for this for many years.) I read the comment section and found most of them to be pretty skeptical of this defense. One said something like, "My dad discovered the cure for any of my 'impulse-control' problems. He said the cure was in my butt and it could be eradicated by several hard swats to it every time it showed up!" The commenter added that it really did cure him as a child. (I'm rather in favor of this treatment in most cases, and I'm thinking his dad could have been my dad's best friend!)

Also, in this case, it was revealed that the child had been enduring this treatment since age 6 and confided that Catrell had always told her it was to be a secret. This recalls the passage where Jesus is speaking to his Disciples about children. In paraphrasing this scripture, He tells them that "anyone who does harm to a child would be 'better off' if they were drowned in the sea". (Matthew 18:6). Not sure what "better off" means, but if I were someone who purposely harmed a child, I would be concerned.

The Good, the Bad and the Ugly:

I have so far written about the many negative results of the '60s 'Revolution', but I am also aware that some good things came from that period. The biggest one was most of the Civil Rights Movement. Previous generations were certainly not innocent of grievous harm, especially to the black citizens of this nation. Due to the Civil Rights Movement, many unfair laws were rightfully changed, and more people became aware of the disparities. Most of the whites-only signs came down, and even inter-marriage and dating began to be a little more acceptable. Still the 'deep' South lagged far behind for many more decades.

Eventually another good thing was the number of TV shows and films that began to include more 'people of color'. I loved the movie *Guess Who's Coming to Dinner* with Sidney Poitier playing the part of a dignified black doctor engaged to a young woman from a typical white family in the '50s. This film was a welcome change to what was usually presented in movies about racial issues. Unfortunately, there will always be bigots in our society, and the Civil Rights Movement is still a 'work-in-progress', but for the most part has been one of the better legacies in my opinion.

I am not so convinced about the forced integration of schools and other government programs, but more about this later.

I also believe the Civil Rights Movement was helpful in bringing about more opportunities for women. The stigma of a 'working mother' began to fade and many jobs that were strictly male-dominated started to be open to women as well. The downside of this is the idea that a woman can do anything as well as a man. Basic physiology trumps that idea! God designed us differently for many reasons and I believe we all would be happier to simply accept this blessing!

Of course, it is great that women can be weightlifters, track athletes, military etc., but it is a rare exception when a female can compete equally with the natural strength and endurance of a male. Why this has become such a debated issue is perplexing, but it is sadly our world today. A lot has been written about this issue, so I will leave this subject to others; and again, feel blessed by my immigrant grandparents for their Christian lifestyle and beliefs that taught me to appreciate the uniqueness of being male or female.

Sex and Rock n' Roll:

The drug era that began in the '60s was a tragic downturn for society, but equally damaging was the 'Sexual Revolution' and some of the music that accompanied it. I liked a lot of the music that came before, during and after 'Woodstock', but it was taking a turn toward a more debased style that was provocative and exciting, but not very supportive of our 'better angels' so to speak. It is easy to see the difference in the music if you watch the programs that feature musicians and performers from an earlier time. Until the late '60s, lyrics were mostly focused on romantic love, life experiences, growing up, and other somewhat innocent subject matter. I'm sure that era looks and sounds corny and old-fashioned to most today. There were no performers who sang (or 'rapped' with profanity) about killing cops, getting high or disrespecting women that are just accepted as part of our music and video entertainment today.

I do believe that the music and movies of today are just a reflection of the reality that sexuality has been reduced to entertainment. This shallow, destructive attitude has created more than one generation that is comfortable with 'shacking up' as well as just being another part of a date! Casual sex has made the experience of true intimacy almost a joke. Believe it or not, before the '60s it was fairly common, especially for girls, to remain a virgin until marriage!

There was a general acceptance that sexual pleasure was the reward of sharing a committed life with someone you loved and wanted to stay with as a lifetime partner. The so-called 'sexual revolution' and rejection of traditional values has been the cause of many broken relationships, unplanned pregnancies, single parenting, incalculable harm to children, millions of aborted babies and the heart-breaking number of fatherless homes!

In addition to the damage caused by the '60s 'if-it-feels-good-do-it' culture, we now have technology that makes pornography available at the click of a mouse or tap of a finger. Engaging in sex with someone of the same gender is also no longer seen as abnormal, and now choosing the gender you think you should be is not only accepted but promoted! Well, if you were fortunate enough to have 'dodged the '60s bullet', you probably agree with me that all this perversion is causing great harm.

Many children are being irreparably damaged by parents who cave to a child's fantasies when they are simply playing or imagining another identity. These parents are guilty of failing to teach their children the reality of their developing bodies. Any doctor or counselor that prescribes a sex change for a child should lose their license to practice! I am forever grateful that my daughter did not fall for this current nonsense and assume anything when we witnessed an outburst from her son. He had come home from school and seemed a little irritated. He was about 7 years old, and his mom asked him what was wrong. He shouted, "I wish I was a *girl*!" When we both asked why, he loudly declared: "'Cause…they always get to go *FIRST*!"

Maybe asking questions might prevent a child from possible manipulation. I know for a fact that if my child *seriously* expressed a belief they wanted to be (or thought they should be) the opposite sex, I would be spending a *LOT* of time asking questions until I was convinced that they truly understood what they were talking about. I would want to know why they were having these thoughts and make sure they understood the possible consequences of acting on their beliefs. (Being unhappy that Mom or Dad won't indulge their belief that they are a puppy is not nearly as serious as indulging their belief that they are not the gender their body says they are.)

I remember the times when my grandson, still in elementary school, wanted to wear my blue sequined high heels around the house. Not once did I or my daughter think he was a possible 'trans' in need of a sex change!

We are now learning that many children that age and younger are being diagnosed with being in the wrong body, in need of hormones and even surgery to become the opposite sex! This is often based solely on a little boy's desire to try on his sister's dress or put on makeup, or a girl who hates to wear dresses. These assumptions are truly evil, and I will accuse any parent of child abuse if they see these behaviors as anything other than normal during childhood.

I knew many girls when I was growing up that loved to play cowboys and Indians, wore boy's clothes, and pretended to be Superman or some other male character! Most were called 'tomboys'. They eventually grew into their femininity, and it was never a life-changing issue. This is truly a destructive social trend that promotes the idea that gender is a matter of choice and not our God-given biology.

Along with the subject of transgenderism, there are also some very real issues with most who identify as gay. Every gay person I have known has told me they were sexually or emotionally abused as children. One sweet man I had for a friend acquired AIDS from his partner. He was cared for by a doctor who was also a Pastor of a Christian church. This doctor treated him with a medical regime that gave my friend five more years of life than expected. At some point in his treatment, he accepted Christ as his savior and confided in me about his 'decision' to be gay. He told me that his mother had been a prostitute, and he had experienced so much abuse himself that he was afraid he might also abuse any children that might result from a relationship with a woman.

Tammy Bruce, a prominent author, and conservative commentator on Fox News is very open about her 'choice' to be gay. In one of her books, she states that her choice was simply because she is 'more comfortable' with other women. I don't believe she has expressed anything more about this, and I respect her honesty as well as her great writing and news commentary. (It would be interesting to know why she feels 'less comfortable with men' though.) I also had a former friend/roommate, Darla, who had a lot of confusion about her sexuality and was also *extremely* promiscuous with men. After her father passed away, she went into grief counseling because she wanted to understand why she refused to attend his funeral. Darla was in her 50s at this time when she finally faced the suppressed reality that he had sexually abused her from age two until her late teens!

This woman had not dodged the '60s bullet. We had met years before as co-workers when I was about 28 and she was 7 years younger. At that time, she was an avid astrologist, expert Tarot-card reader, New-Ager, and yoga enthusiast. Darla was the epitome of a 'Woodstock Hippy': free-spirited, mostly fun to be around and highly intelligent. We eventually went our separate ways after she faced the truth about her father. I hope she is okay somewhere now, as she used to tell me she often saw demons in her rear-view mirror when driving at night! Even though I wasn't much of a Christian then, I somehow avoided the danger of dabbling too much in the dark side with her.

I am not an expert on matters of perverse sexual harm, only offering my observations that these trends and social attitudes are not adding anything positive to our already fallen human condition and life choices.

Chapter 6
RACIAL ISSUES, SYSTEMIC and OTHERWISE

In addition to sexual issues, another well-intentioned effort to be 'liberally progressive, tolerant and inclusive' in the name of civil rights has backfired big time! That would be the Affirmative Action programs that have done more to damage race relations than was ever thought possible. And yes, I do have a 'dog' in this fight.

My older brother was a truly gifted artist, hard-working and dedicated to always doing his best. When he had completed twenty years of military service at age 39, he was ready to rejoin the civilian work force. He was highly decorated for his position in the military and applied for a job in a career that was ideal for his skills and experience. He took additional College classes in order to meet the requirement for technological proficiency in that position. The application process included three separate interviews for each applicant, and he was told that he had scored the highest at that point.

I know how elated he was during this process, and I know how devastated he was when he told me why he was denied the position. The hiring manager, apparently against the rules of confidentiality, told my brother that although he was the most qualified, the company was required to hire a minority.

This resulted in my brother becoming so discouraged that he suffered from depression. He eventually accepted a minimum-wage job that he kept until he retired.

In my opinion this policy, in the name of equal or civil rights, *is* racism in its most hypocritical form! It is also SYSTEMIC racism as it is still being applied today! This policy is completely insulting as it implies that if someone is not white, they cannot be expected to be qualified for a job on their own merits! Nobody wants to be hired because of a quota for their race. How demeaning, unjust and racist this is!

No Prejudice Allowed Here:

Despite these policies and the treatment of my brother, there is no animosity toward any race in my family. This is another blessing from my Christian grandparents. I recall many lectures from my grandfather (and my dad) regarding any form of prejudice. Maybe because we were German, we were told to be especially conscious of our attitudes towards our Jewish neighbors as well. There was an Italian Jewish family across the street, but our area had no black, Asian or Hispanic families that I know of. All I know is that we were never taught that our white race was superior in any way to others. My dad worked with several black and Asian men at his various jobs and always spoke well of them. His bowling league was also 'diverse', and they called themselves *The Mixed Nuts*. They would often go out for drinks after bowling, and my dad always tried to foot the bill!

My own experience with 'diversity' during my teens was when I was asked to babysit for a Jewish couple who lived a few blocks away. They were both medical doctors and had two school- age children. Their home was well-kept, and the children seemed happy and well-behaved. Whenever I babysat, the kids always tried to con me into staying up late, but I followed their parents' rules and did not relent. I always made sure the house was clean and dishes were washed as part of my job. After babysitting several more times, the mom asked me to be a server at a meeting they were planning to have at their house. It was going to be catered and I was to wear a black skirt and a white blouse. I was about 14 and had never done anything like this but told her I was willing.

Now that I look back, I have to think these Jewish people were also not prejudiced. Many are (justifiably) and are wary of 'Gentiles' because of what they have suffered under so-called Christians and others in the past. Sadly, today there is still a lot of anti-Semitism that is rearing its head again. This mostly stems from the mistaken belief that only the Jews were responsible for the crucifixion of Jesus. There is on-going hatred from the teachings of Islam that claim the Jewish race is inferior and should be eliminated. Many others believe that Jews control everything to enrich their own; and they are only successful because they are dishonest and greedy by nature! Then there was Adolf Hitler, a German dictator who did his best to teach that and kill as many as possible. He succeeded in killing more than 6 million with the help of many so-called Christian German citizens. We can even go back to ancient history and read about their 400 years of slavery by the Egyptians, and further back in the Bible to understand God's covenant with Abraham and the significance of his two sons.

Brother from Another Mother:

The racial hatred and religious conflict that continues today between the Jews and the Arabs began with the birth of Ishmael (Genesis 16). The following account is paraphrased and condensed to make a long story short.

Abraham and his wife, Sarai (later called Sarah) had been promised by God to have a son, but they lost faith after being past child-bearing age. She decided to offer her servant, Hagar, to Abraham (not an unusual practice) in order to bear him a son. Abraham and his wife were both Jewish, but Hagar was an Egyptian-Arab.

God was not pleased with this whole decision, but Hagar also prayed for a blessing. An angel of the Lord appeared to her and told her she was going to bear a male child, and to call him Ishmael and he would be the 'father' of many. Scripture says he would be a 'wild donkey of a man whose hand will be against everyone; and his descendants will live to the east of all his brothers'. They became the Arab nations. Years later God fulfilled his promise to give Abraham a son through his *wife* and to name him Isaac. His descendants would be the 'chosen' people of Israel with their numbers being 'too many to count'. However, when Isaac was a young adult God tested Abraham's faith by commanding him to sacrifice his only divinely-promised son.

This is a difficult scenario to make sense of because without Isaac there would be no 'chosen' people! Well, scripture does tell us that God also said, *"My thoughts are not your thoughts, and my ways are not your ways"* (Isaiah 55:8). So I will leave it at that. Abraham did obey as commanded, but before he could kill his son the angel of the Lord stopped him and told him he would find a ram nearby that was caught in a thicket to use for the sacrifice (Gen. 22:10-13). Most Bible scholars view this account as the foretelling of the eventual sacrifice of Christ (the unblemished *'Lamb'*) the only begotten son of God.

To sum things up, there was bad blood between Isaac and Ishmael as God's covenant was only with Abraham and his descendants through Isaac. The Arabs viewed Ishmael as the rightful heir to receive God's promise to Abraham, and this is still the case today. 500 years after Christ, Muhammad arrived and claimed this view of Ishmael as the 'truth', fostering the mistaken claim that Israel belonged to the Muslim Arabs. This is the major danger to the tiny Jewish State, but there is also the on-going hatred and prejudice against them in our nation and others as well.

Maybe the Jewish family I babysat for was lucky enough to have grandparents like mine who taught them God's truth, that we are all only one race—*human*—and therefore had no problem trusting a second generation German girl like me!

I never did find out what kind of a gathering I was serving at that day, but the guests were highly professional and very gracious as I came by with trays of foods that were strange to me. In the kitchen the catering lady asked me if I wanted to sample what she said were 'lox and bgaels. They were little doughnut shaped, dense breads, cut crossways with crème cheese and thin slices of smoked salmon on them. What a treat it was! It might seem odd to not be familiar with this food, but back then in Seattle there were very few places to enjoy foods from different cultures. We did occasionally go to what was called 'China Town' south of downtown for the incredible food that was served in those restaurants. The owners and servers were so friendly, and the atmosphere was always like a party!

Today we are blessed with an amazing variety of international foods to choose from in even the smallest towns. (I must admit I could eat Mexican food every day.) America has been truly blessed by the many ethnic peoples that chose to become 'out of many one'! If we were just a nation of European and Nordic 'pale-faces' I'm afraid we would not have the great artwork, literature, science, music, theater, sports (or foods) we enjoy today!

Culture, Race and Birds of a Feather:

In my senior year, the first black student was welcomed into our all-white school. He was a big guy and was immediately put on the football team. As a novelty, he was also befriended right away. If anyone was harboring some prejudice it could not have lasted long because he acted just like the white guys!

It wasn't that there were no blacks living in Seattle at the time, it's just that they mostly lived in the south end of the city and went to black-majority schools. In fact, our biggest game of the year was with our arch-rival, the all-black football team of Garfield High. They usually beat us, but it was the best entertainment! Their marching band and cheerleaders always got the highest awards every year as well. They were also the strongest competitor in our annual jazz festivals and usually beat us there too!

Even though there was a form of segregation in the schools and neighborhoods, it seemed almost voluntary and acceptable at that time, at least in the area I grew up in. (Actually, I sometimes wonder if it might be more of a 'birds-of-a-feather-flock-together' thing than a racial thing.) Anyway, most black families then were as traditional as most white families, and many were also just as dysfunctional as many whites were. Even our history shows the statistics that support this. So why and when did things change for the worse?

Everything changed after the Civil Rights Movement exposed the unequal treatment of blacks, especially in the South. I, personally, have never met anyone who thought this was anything but evil! Tragically, the thing that has done the most damage to our black population is the War on Poverty instigated by President Johnson in 1964. This disastrous, but *supposedly* well-meaning, effort to correct the perception and realities of unequal outcomes started with a program that rewarded women for having children as long as they were not married or had any adult male living with them! Cash, food stamps, housing and healthcare were available if you followed the government rules!

It was not long before the term 'Welfare Queen' was heard, and resentments (now labeled racism) started to bubble up. But this situation was true for many poor white families as well! These programs damaged untold numbers of children as well as the men who were encouraged to stay out of their lives. Too many men then decided to just make babies and had several 'baby mamas' they would visit once a month for their 'share' of the money and other 'benefits'. (I have seen this up-close and personal in my lifetime and it continues today.) The results of fatherless homes are well documented and a major cause of crime, substance abuse, child neglect and even illiteracy! I keep hoping America will realize just how damaging these policies are and vote to change them!

The biggest misconception behind these programs is the belief that poverty causes crime. I have known many 'poor' people who were honest, dependable, and hard-working, and there is also no shortage of well-off folks who would sell their own mother to get what they want! All you need to do is read the daily news to see how many highly paid heads of charities are caught ripping off the donations! How about some of the so-called 'public servants' we trust and elect to manage these tax-funded programs?

The truth is *crime and immorality* cause poverty! It is a problem of *character*, not wealth, and with all due respect to Anne Frank, people are *not* 'really good at heart'! You do not have to be a genius to see this truth. The human inclination to be self-centered jerks can be easily seen if you would just watch a room full of toddlers for about a half hour! Or, if not that, ask yourself if you can remember when you taught your child to lie! (Trust me; it comes as natural as breathing.) *"All have sinned…"* (Romans 3:23) *"…there is none good"* (Matthew 19:17).

If we *were* born good, I wonder if we would even *have* the free will to act badly?

'People of Color' in My Life:

Two of my grandchildren are 'black' (mixed like Obama), with my German/Scandinavian/British daughter being their mom, and their dad being of African and possibly Native American descent. They do not fit any kind of stereotype and are both functioning adults that I love deeply. And yes, they both got 'the talk' just like their white mom got about respecting the police. Now that I might have earned the right to claim I am not a racist, I would like to share my experiences with other 'people of color' (the good and the bad).

My first personal encounter with a black man was when I was about 27 years old. I was working as a hostess/cashier in a small but classy hotel dining room. He was about 80 years old and had his own shoe-shine business in the hallway next to the hotel barber shop. His name was Jackie Green, and although he has long since passed on, I will never forget him.

Every morning he would come into the waiting area of the dining room and go to the breakfast counter for a cup of coffee. He would always come up to me to pay for it. I tried to tell him that he was a hotel employee and did not need to pay for coffee. He answered in his slow, southern country drawl, telling me "No, ma'am, I always pays my way!"

In relating the following conversation, I'm choosing to use his manner of speaking to convey his warm and disarming personality.

It was another typical morning when Mr. Green came up to pay for his coffee. This time he touched the back of my hand and said, "Missy, you gots the gift o' wisdom, and I wants to tell ya' somethin' that'll he'p you all yer life!"

I said, "Okay, Mr. Green."

He looked straight at me and continued with: "Always remember… when folks is busy tellin' you what they is, tha's likely what they ain't, and when they's busy tellin' you what they ain't, tha's likely what they is!"

I believe the key word in his advice was "busy", and I learned through the years just how true it has proven to be!

I eventually left that job after about seven years, and I think he was still working at his shoeshine stand then. If I believed that humans could become angels, I would think he had to be one now! But wait…doesn't scripture state that we might *entertain angels unaware*?

Well, sure enough, that would be Hebrews 13:2! Actually, angels *can* appear as humans, but they are separate beings created before humans, and we cannot become one…Genesis 1:26. (Sorry, Clarence, you were so lovable in *It's a Wonderful Life!*)

Along with my old black friend, I had additional experience with 'people of color' at my hotel job. They were the Korean, Chinese and Thailand co-workers I spent forty hours a week with. The male waiters were mostly Thailand college students studying engineering at the University of Washington. Most started out as busboys and worked up to being waiters. They could speak enough English to get by and some of them were very fun to be around, as well as hard-working. (Only one was kind of a jerk and not well-liked by the others.) Several hotel guests asked me if this hotel dining room was a Chinese restaurant, but I explained that the waiters were all UW students who had friends that wanted to work here and they soon became the whole crew.

The breakfast and lunch staff consisted of several white females, one white male waiter and one white busboy. There was one Korean male who told me he was trying to save enough money to bring his wife here. These guys were great to work with, and to top it off, sometime later, a young Chinese immigrant from Hong Kong was hired. (This young man would later become the best boss I ever had!)

Lee was just 16 when he was hired as a busboy. He could only speak Chinese but was an incredible worker. The older head waitress decided to take him under her wing so he could learn the 'ropes' as well as some English. He was a fast learner and was soon speaking English well enough to start waiting on tables.

The hotel also offered room service and Lee was eventually allowed to do this as well. It was part of my job to take the calls for room service and before too long I realized the overwhelming requests were for Lee to be the one to serve them! Management was also noticing Lee's performance, and he was soon promoted to head waiter. During the dinner shifts that I occasionally worked, I got to witness Lee's style up close.

After a few times watching him work the dining room, I thought well, no wonder; if this was how he treated the room service orders, I can understand the requests! The thing that made him so different from the average room service waiter was that he presented the meal with the same grace and elegance as he did in the dining room. Most room servers would just enter the room, put the trays on the table and leave. Lee would engage the guests in polite conversation while setting the table with a clean cloth and utensils. (He also never forgot any possible condiments that might be needed.) When all was ready, he would pull out a chair to seat any lady in the room before serving.

Lee was never a show-boat type of waiter, just respectful and thoughtful with attention to every detail. By his third year, he was appointed dining room manager, and this is when it really got 'real'. I was expected to attend all the meetings he called for the dining room staff. It was during the first meeting that I realized how gifted he was in getting the best out of everyone.

It might be helpful to visualize what this hotel dining room was like. The decor was designed with an Old-English motif. There were about eight round tables that could each seat four or more, and several large and small booths with wooden dividers that provided some privacy between. The chairs were on wheels and all seating was upholstered like the overstuffed furniture you might find in a private library. The lights were dimmed for the dinner shift and the tables covered with patterned Damask cloths and linen napkins. Each table had a real candle in a brass lamp that added a pleasant glow to the room. The background music was soft, and kitchen noise could not be heard unless you were in the breakfast-counter area. In other words, a welcoming, charming place to dine!

No matter how pricy or elegant a restaurant is, we have all experienced a less than wonderful time; I know I have. It seems that Lee was aware of this as well because it became obvious that he was not going to allow that to be the case on *his* watch!

Even though Lee's English was limited, there was no doubt as to his message. At the first staff meeting I heard him, in his Asian accent, declare the following: "Most important thing! Every customer KING and QUEEN! No matter come for coffee or bowl of soup! Can come back with WHOLE FAMILY for steak dinner! Treat all SAME!"

Next were the directives about the room: "All tables spotless, all seats and floors clean of dust and crumbs! Every salt and pepper full and clean, all utensil no smudge! No tablecloth with stain! All napkins folded same! Table lamps clean with new candle!" Of course, he also instructed (and demonstrated) the proper way to attend each guest while serving. All I know is after these meetings I was ready to crawl through broken glass to do my part! (Trust me; I made sure the menus I took to each table were spotlessly clean as well.) If every boss could inspire and instill pride to get the best from their staff the way Lee did, we would all be much happier in our jobs, in my opinion!

I worked there for a few more years, and by the time I left, Lee had become not just the dining room manager, but the manager of the hotel, and then the entire small chain, including a hotel in Portland. I don't believe Lee's race had anything to do with his success. He was successful because of hard work, dedication, and personal ethics; otherwise known as *character.*

Come to think of it, the most successful agencies or businesses I worked for had managers like Lee, and I'm convinced that people who have started from the bottom always make the best bosses! (Actually, they all seemed to follow that 'golden rule' of treating others the way *they* would like to be treated!)

The Bad Apples:

The reason I know it is not race but character can be illustrated by my interaction with another 'person-of-color'. This was a second generation Chinese female I worked with at the hotel. Irene was very beautiful, intelligent, and charming. She was hard-working and spoke perfect English. She was also a devious, back-stabbing, arrogant ladder-climber! (I'm not always good at holding back an assessment.) Irene wanted to take Lee's place, and I watched how she treated the rest of the staff. She seemed to favor only one of the waitresses: a sweet, quiet blonde named Lisa who doted on her every move. Irene was aloof to the rest; unlike Lee who was always respectful and friendly to *everyone.*

Irene was also fond of holding little 'seminars' in her apartment where she could lecture all of us with her wisdom and superior attributes. ('Humble' is not an adjective that comes to mind with Irene.) I would say she was also an expert at using what we now call micro-aggressions. Back-handed 'compliments' from her were common, and she seemed to know nothing about constructive criticism either.

The only admiration I thought she deserved would be for the professional, gracious way she dealt with the hotel owners and guests. (No motive there, I'm sure.) All in all, Irene was the kind of person you never felt at ease around unless you were in her 'circle'… and she did have one.

The Invitation:

Sometime after working at the hotel for several years, my 14-year-old marriage ended. I had always kept my personal life private, but eventually the staff heard about it. An upper-level manager even complimented me for 'keeping it separate from the job'.

At some point after this was known, I was invited to a party Irene was having. The invitation came from her favorite waitress, Lisa. Being a recently divorced mom of a 9-year-old, I was not in any frame of mind for a party, but Lisa kept insisting over the next several days until I finally agreed.

I arranged for childcare, bought a bottle of wine and a small bouquet, and left for the party. Someone answered the door, and I went in. There were many guests, and I spotted Lisa chatting with several women in the entry area, but she did not acknowledge me. I saw several waiters with Lee quietly talking in the living room area. I was still standing by the door when I heard Irene (who was in the kitchen, surrounded by several young men) calling out, "Well, what do you know; here comes the cashier who was not invited but shows up anyway!"

It must have been about two or three seconds before I set the wine and flowers down on the entry-way table and left.

When I came to work on Monday, I saw Lisa, but she gave no sign that she even knew I had tried to attend the party, and no awareness of Irene's reaction whatsoever. I started to wonder if it had just been an unpleasant dream! I eventually told my Tarot-card-reading-Hippy friend, Darla, about the experience.

For all her faults, Darla was so wicked-smart; you would pay any amount to have her as your defense attorney! Scripture describes the tongue as 'a *two-*

edged sword'. Well, Darla's tongue had extremely sharp edges! I have yet to meet anyone since with a vocabulary as extensive as hers; combined with a vocal style of such silky venom that when she was finished you knew you were too!

I did not witness her intervention; I only know that Irene avoided me at all costs from that time forward. Lisa and I just remained co-workers as before. Strangely enough, after my time at the hotel was over, I got a Christmas photo-card from Lisa. She had married a Chinese man and they had an adorable little boy! (Did she really not remember the party episode?) Oh well, I wished her the best.

As for Irene, 'bad apples' are in every race because they are the *exceptions*. They should never be used to defend a bigoted viewpoint. Again, isn't it always about character?

Children and Racism:

When I was in my fifties, I was living in a Condo. There was a neighbor across from my unit who had a little blonde girl, Siri, around 3 years old. I had temporary custody of my granddaughter, Sasha, at the time. (Sasha is half black and was about the same age.) The girls soon started to play together. They were especially happy when putting my cat in a doll stroller, wrapped in a blanket, pushing it up and down the hallway. After a while I started making simple dinners for both girls when I got home from work, and eventually Siri's mom, Carol, would come over to visit as well.

One evening Carol said she wanted to tell me about an incident that had worried her. She said that Siri had asked her something about me and Sasha, saying: "Mommy; they're the dark people and we're the light people, right?" Carol said she immediately thought, 'Oh boy, here we go with the race thing!' Then, with a smile, told me that after a short pause, Siri continued with: "… 'cause they have dark hair and we have blonde hair, right?"

Children are not racists! Racism must be taught. I have watched many 'diverse' groups of toddlers at daycare playing together, and the desire to maim each other over a toy applies to every race equally. *Truth!*

Bigotry is a learned attitude, and I eventually had to explain that to my own child when she started kindergarten.

My husband and I had been married about nine years when we moved into a wonderful, diverse neighborhood where our daughter, Claire, would be one of the few white children in the elementary school. Crazy as this might sound, 5-year-old Claire walked the several blocks to and from there every day. (Like I did at that age…sigh, a different time.)

On her first day of school when I got home from work, I asked her how the day went. She looked upset and told me some boys had called her names when she was walking home. When I asked her what kind of names, her eyes welled up before she said, "They were yelling 'Honky, Honky'!" I asked her what she did then; she said, "I yelled back, 'Honky *YOU!*'"

I stifled my urge to smile and told her that was perfectly okay for her to do and to just ignore them and make friends with the nice kids. Since that was the only time it happened, her response must have made an impact. Most likely they just thought she was clueless (which she thankfully was). Her class had several black, Hispanic, and Asian kids, and she never seemed to have any bad days after that.

Our street was multi-racial as well. Next door to our right was an Irish couple, on the left were two older ladies from somewhere in Eastern Europe that I would often see using a small brush to scrub their outside window trims with! Next to them was an Italian family whose youngest son liked to play with Claire despite how much younger he was. Across the street was a Vietnamese family with two little girls Claire would play with as well. When I would go there to get her after work, their dad would be sitting on the floor with all of them, usually playing a game. He was very friendly but could not speak English. The girls came to Claire's birthday party every year and were always sweet and polite. The only black mixed family was further down the street. The mom was black, the dad white, and their two kids were unusually beautiful. Another great thing about this area was the best grocery store you could ever hope for! It had the most amazing variety of foods, and I wish I were still living in that neighborhood. Unfortunately, that area of Seattle is no longer affordable unless you are blessed with an upper-class income. The saddest thing is why can't every neighborhood be mixed as naturally as this was?

The Elephant in the Room:

I can't help but conclude that race is not the issue our major media (and academia) focuses on. Someone taught those little boys to think their treatment of another child was justified because of her race. As illustrated previously, children are not born racist!

Another incident I remember happened at a high-end car dealership I was working in. I was an office assistant and was asked to purge the auto service files. I had boxed them up for storage and hoped I could find one of the guys to help move them down the hall. I spotted a young man in the break room and asked if he could help me. His name was Devon and had just been hired as a lot helper. He was a teen, like the others who started out this way in the dealership. He seemed a little unsure but was willing to help me out. Later that day I saw him again, and he told me he had gotten in trouble with his supervisor. He said he was told he had to do better at his job and be more available with the crew. Then he added: "I think it's just 'cause I'm black."

I decided to confront his supervisor, Sam, with what Devon had told me, and to explain that I had asked him to help me with moving some boxes. I found Sam and told him that Devon believed he was in trouble because he was black. I said it was my fault he was not with the crew during the time he was helping me. Sam asked me to step into his office to discuss the situation. He told me that Devon was not in trouble for helping me and it had nothing to do with him being black. He went on to explain that Devon had been caught several times sleeping in the vehicles and leaving his service pager off so he couldn't be reached when needed.

Sam said that he would be giving Devon another chance to improve but would have to let him go if it happened again. Unfortunately, it did happen again, and Devon was fired. I felt bad for him, but I knew one thing for sure; someone had taught Devon that his race would be the reason (or excuse) for any problems he might have in life. This happened in the '90s, but here in the year 2020, Devon would very likely sue the dealership for discrimination because our society still refuses to see the elephant in the room!

The elephant is *nurture*, not nature! Any child brought up to think their race matters more than their character is damaged! This was another 'bullet' from the '60s when the liberal leaders were telling minorities that they were just victims of a white majority. Even though so much has improved for every ethnic group since then, the policies that were put in place are still causing devastating harm, and the same leaders are still calling them victims.

I mentioned earlier I would relate the disaster that came from forced busing in the '70s. This was supposed to 'integrate' and improve education for black children. Instead, *all* kids suffered from this! My friend Sally and her husband had purchased a home in the school district they wanted for their kids. Later that same year they were told their girls would be bussed almost 20 miles away to an inner-city school so that 'disadvantaged' kids could attend the school they had wanted for their girls. This would mean hours on a bus and no time with friends in their own neighborhood, as well as almost no parent-teacher involvement. They decided to sell their home and move to a county where this was not happening. Sally and her husband had no issue with 'children of color', but they and anyone else who protested the bussing were labeled racists. Many parents followed suit and this reaction came to be called 'White Flight'.

The black kids were just as unhappy as the white kids! Being so far from their homes and their peers was not at all conducive to a better education! There were fights on the buses and more bullying in school than before. Students could not participate in after-school activities and had no time for community involvement. Discipline issues were compounded by the difficulty of parent-teacher interaction, yet this policy was enforced for decades. We are *still* paying a high price for this mistake!

If all the difficulties for 'people of color' were really because of racism, how did Dr. Ben Carson happen? How is it we voted in a black president for two terms? How did a black man become the first surgeon to perform a heart transplant? How do we have several non-whites on the Supreme Court? How did Oprah become one of the most admired and wealthy black females in the world? I cannot list every incredibly smart, talented, brave, or gifted non-white person here as that would fill a book bigger than a dictionary! I know that very few came from a background of privilege, but they all had one thing in common: they chose to believe they could succeed regardless of race. I wish Ben Carson's book, *You Have a Brain*, was required reading from grade five and up! Another one would be Supreme Court Justice Clarence Thomas's book, *My Grandfather's Son.* These books describe everything one needs to know about true racism, but also how important our upbringing is in shaping each of us.

Racism on Steroids:

To believe that racial discrimination was not a horrific issue after slavery was abolished in America would be utter denial and dangerously ignorant. The problem since the '60s is the guilt and shame that promotes policies that do not help! Shelby Steele wrote a book titled *White Guilt*. He had been part of a radical organization, the Black Panthers. These young men would go onto college campuses and barge into the admin offices and demand changes they were adamant about. They were extremely disrespectful, doing things like putting out their cigarettes in the office carpets and threatening the college deans with worse if their demands were not met. At some point during that time, Shelby came to realize that their intimidating tactics were only working because of the guilt of the mostly white people they were confronting. The subtitle of his book is '*How BLACKS & WHITES Together DESTROYED the PROMISE of the CIVIL RIGHTS ERA*'. He had also written a best seller titled *The Content of Our Character*. If I could mandate these books for required reading for every high school, I would do it!

There have been several times since when students have staged unjustified, obnoxious, disrespectful 'sit-ins' and demonstrations that did not help much in the way of productive change. But incredibly, we now have racism on steroids! There are now two new efforts the race-baiting social justice folks have invented called 'White Privilege' and 'Critical Race Theory'. These movements are currently being accepted as worthy to receive money to fund seminars with forced attendance in government and private sector jobs. These race-based intimidation seminars should never be tolerated in any form. Forcing any person to confess, confirm or agree they are a racist just because they were born with light colored skin is the epitome of bigotry!

About ten years ago, I was working part time in a non-profit agency for women and children who needed help in leaving abusive relationships. I assisted in prepping the rooms and doing some clerical duties. Most of the staff was college age white women, with one white male, but there was one older black lady who retired while I was there. I liked everyone and always had a good rapport with the families staying there. Many were Hispanic and a few were black, but most were white. One afternoon I was asked to go out for coffee with one of the young staffers. She explained that the purpose was to discuss my 'white privilege'. This was the first time I had heard the term but was fine with learning what she meant. I don't remember mentioning my two half-black grandchildren who were living with me at that time; I only remember being told how important it was for me to realize how blind all white people are to their 'in-born racism'.

Fast forward to 2020, and this movement along with 'Critical Race Theory' has become so insulting and racist that President Trump issued an Executive Order to ban it from being presented in any federal workplace! This is still being welcomed in many private businesses and mandated that only *whites* are to attend! I can only imagine how this would affect morale, especially for the non-whites that work there! How humiliating to be singled out and treated with this disrespect while making an issue of their skin color or ethnic origins! How did any of this thinking become acceptable in this country? Maybe we need to be re-educated about the Christian foundation of this nation and the fact that there is NO racism in Christian beliefs. Cultural and racial differences are mentioned in the Bible only to clarify or describe an event, but never to denigrate a race!

God's 'Word' teaches NOTHING about racial superiority other than explaining a cultural belief like the attitude towards Samaritans by the Jews at that time. We were each created in the 'image' of God (meaning a reflection of His character), but because of human rebellion, and by our own choices, we fall very short of that attribute! Anyone who thinks the Bible teaches racism is completely ignorant, and if claiming to be Christian needs to get into spiritual rehab ASAP or risk being correctly labeled a CINO (Christian in name only)! In ending this chapter, I pray that this current effort to further divide us and foster even more bigotry is never accepted! We need to be vigilant. We need to speak out publicly and teach our children the truth! We need to stop politicians and educators from promoting these ideas. Standing by and doing nothing when we see this kind of evil makes us guilty of endorsing it!

Chapter 7
'EQUAL' CULTURES and GETTING 'WOKE'

Maybe I should explain about the term *'woke'* (liberal slang for awake or aware). It was originally intended to mean that a person or policy was progressive, inclusive, non-racist, culturally aware and sophisticated. But because of the hypocrisy and just plain nonsense in its use, it has become a term of well-deserved derision and mockery. (The following is just a further personal illustration of why.)

Included with the previously mentioned 'white-privilege' consultation at the shelter, I was also expected to have enthusiastic respect and admiration for all cultures. (There was a sign or poster in every entryway proclaiming this policy in one manner or another.) And this was not the only agency I worked in that made this policy a priority of employment, and I soon experienced a situation that occurred because of it.

Sometime after the attack on the twin towers in 2001, a few employees were discussing their opinions in the break room. Someone mentioned that although the attack was carried out by Arab Muslim men, we had to remember that their culture still deserved respect. I could not hold back.

The remark was from a young woman, and I said, "Excuse me…I don't believe a culture that cuts off a woman's fingers if she is seen wearing nail polish is a culture that deserves respect." There were looks of shock and outrage in the faces of the whole group. (Now that I am reflecting on this, it occurs to me that I was probably the only person working there without a 'woke' college degree!) When another one brought up the idea that the Muslim faith was equal to Christianity, I could not help myself, again. I reminded them of the Muslim practice of stoning women to death if caught in adultery. I went on to describe the story of Jesus who stopped the stoning of a woman who was guilty of the same (John 8:1-30). Two of the young women listening seemed very pleased to hear this story. They especially liked the part where Jesus tells her she was *'forgiven and free to go'*, but when I mentioned that he also told her to *'go and sin no more'* well, I can only say they were not happy anymore.

Later that day, I got called into my supervisor's office.

Sasha and Siri 1996

1973 Beacon Hill. Claire with her Vietnam friends at their house after school (Seattle) age 5

Claire's Asian friends at her b party

1st day of kindergarten 1997

check the doll choices

1972 Me & Claire

Claire age 2

Claire 4yrs. old

Sasha age 4

The supervisor was a very smart, highly respected, likeable woman. She told me about the complaint and heard my side of the encounter. She then asked if I had any hard feelings toward the two women that reported it. I answered, "Absolutely not! They had every right to their opinions as I had the right to express mine." She then smiled and thanked me before I went back to my desk. There were no further issues with the two who had been offended, or at least, I was never aware of any. (Sadly, it seems liberals believe they are obliged to report someone they disagree with to a superior…a growing 'woke' thing that only further divides us!)

In addition to the above is the continuing result of the '60s attitude that there should be little or no consequences for immoral or even criminal behavior. This has become a major part of our social ills. This attitude is accepted as proof of how 'woke' we are. It starts with 'time-out' parenting and continues through K-12 and higher education. Even people who call themselves Christian have fallen for the idea that we are not to ever be judgmental or punitive.

This is such a far cry from the Bible teachings on this subject, but I want to address these kinds of misconceptions in another chapter. The problem with the belief that being 'woke' means you are non-judgmental and therefore morally superior falls apart because of its hypocrisy.

The attacks, verbal and sometimes physical, against anyone who does not agree with the 'woke' are blatant proof of that lie. They will de-friend you, boycott your business, harass and instigate all forms of *judgment*, including the rioting and destruction we have witnessed for all of 2020 and continuing! This is only one example of how concepts and actions that are just plain stupid, harmful or evil are revealed by the greatest revealer of all…*HYPOCRICSY!*

'Woke' is probably one of the most idiotic terms to be invented, let alone accepted, in my lifetime! However, the following is my experience relating to this term as *I* prefer to use it.

Getting Woke on 9-11:

My neighbor, Carol, woke me up out of a sound sleep early in the morning of September 11th, 2001. She lived across the hall from me in the condo where her child played with my granddaughter who was living with me. I was recovering from cancer surgery and was not happy about waking up at all!

She apologized but said something horrible had happened in New York City and it was on TV. I slowly rolled out of bed, and we went into the living room and turned on the TV. I had to sit carefully on a pillow to protect the recently stitched area of my surgery. Carol made some coffee while I stared at the TV showing what looked like a large passenger plane jammed in the upper level of one of the Twin Towers. Huge black, billowing clouds of smoke and flames were spilling out of the entire area. I thought what a horrible accident and hoped there were no people in that part of the building! The cameras were also starting to show people on the street and commentators were speculating on what had happened.

We watched this for about fifteen minutes as the rescue people were trying to get to the scene when we saw another large plane barrel into the south tower. This was happening in real time in front of our eyes, and I called out "Jesus Christ! What in the hell is happening!" It got worse as we were learning that two other aircraft had been hijacked and one had plowed into the Pentagon with the other still in flight. We eventually heard the frantic communications between the passengers and Air Control before the heroic fight against the hijackers began in one of those planes. That heroic act stopped the mission of this plane by crashing it into a field. There were no survivors.

Over the next few days, information was coming out about the men who did this, who planned it and why. A man named Osama Bin Ladin was said to be behind this attack. I was clueless, so I called the most intelligent, informed person I could think of to get some answers. When Darla picked up the phone, I asked her who Bin Ladin was because they were saying he was behind the 9-11 attack. All she said was, "Oh, they always blame him." Wait…WHAT? *AL-WAYS? THEY?* Why have I never heard of him and what else has he done?

At the age of 50, I could not have been more embarrassed at my ignorance! I had to face the fact that maybe I needed to do more in my spare time than listen to smooth jazz and enjoy some wine after my workday. I realized then it was way past time to get informed and maybe check my spiritual shallowness as well.

The first thing I did was to start listening to talk-radio news programs, including NPR liberal news. As soon as I recovered from my surgery, I bought two books to read. One was the Quran, and the other was a book by a British historian, Bernard Lewis, titled *WHAT WENT WRONG?…The Clash Between Islam and Modernity in the Middle East.*

I found the Quran to be extremely boring but revealing the Muslim religion for its perversion and plagiarism of the Judeo-Christian Bible. It contains some selected teachings from the Old Testament but rejects the deity of Christ. (The Quran was written 500 years after Christ and was possibly dictated by Mohammed's mother.) My real education came from reading Lewis's incredible research and commentaries that explained so clearly the reasons behind the entire Arab hatred of America and almost anything of western values in general. In addition, his book is even more meaningful because it was written *before* 9-11 and without political bias. This book also includes many historical renderings depicting US and British relations with the Arabs, including scenes of the slave markets at that time. He did add an afterward about 9-11 that was insightful as well. I wish his books were also mandatory reading in every school!

I also bought a book on terrorism titled *NEVER AGAIN…Securing America and Restoring Justice* by John Ashcroft, the former Attorney General serving during the time of 9-11. I continued to read many other books related to current events, history, and politics in general. The best part of getting 'woke' was dusting off the Bible I was given by a co-worker I used to banter with about Christianity before I left that job. It is an NRV study edition, and it is now a bit tattered with lots of highlighting and side comments as well as sticky notes hanging on the edges of many pages. What continues to amaze and frustrate me more these days is the WILLFUL ignorance of way too many people, even though I was so guilty of it myself! I recall the scripture that warns of ignoring information, found in Hosea 4:6. In so many words it states that God's people *'are perishing for their lack of knowledge'*. Meaning they are suffering and even in danger of losing eternal life because they have rejected His truth and guidance. I believe we are all responsible for discerning the truth about events and trends we see happening around us, regardless of our culture or religion. Those who obscure the truth or lie by omitting information are most likely *'perishing'* as well. Unless they stop and fully understand how serious this is, there will be more political and social damage that they will not want to answer to God for.

After learning more about the 9-11 attack, I remembered an Islam-related issue a co-worker told me about. One of the receptionists at the dealership I was working in had become friendly enough to share personal info. This friendship with Jackie started with my envy of the incredibly wonderful lunches her husband made for her! I had never seen such delicious and artistic open-faced baguette sandwiches in my life! She explained that he was just using food choices he was used to in his home country of Morocco. The first sandwich I saw had sliced chicken with shredded lettuce, sliced red onions, topped with chopped celery, apple slices, walnuts, raisins, and feta cheese. Others were of various meats or sea foods and cheeses, with a variety of toppings like black olives, fresh spinach or cucumbers, mushrooms and sliced hard boiled eggs. Some looked like a long pizza and could be microwaved if preferred warm! (Too many to list here before it should be a chapter on sandwich recipes!) In addition to her great lunches, Jackie was always fun to talk with. She was a happy person with a good sense of humor as well.

I asked her how she met this wonderful Arabic man, and she said it happened while she was studying in Morocco. He proposed and wanted to live in America with her, so they married and now had a 12-year-old son. Jackie was pleased that I admired the culinary talent of her mate, and when I asked her if she knew how blessed she was, she just smiled. It was unusual for her to be in a serious mood, but during one of our lunch breaks she told me about an issue with her son that was not a happy one. The boy had asked her and his dad if he could go to a neighborhood Mosque to learn about Islam. Neither of them was a practicing Muslim as far as I knew, but they were fine with him learning about it…until they weren't.

Jackie said it was all good until their son started to criticize the way she dressed. He told her she needed to wear more modest outfits and to stop using makeup. She then described her husband's reaction. She prefaced that by informing me that "This *A-rab*" (as she affectionately referred to him at times) was nobody to mess with if something was important to him! She said he yanked their son out of that Mosque immediately and made it completely clear that there would be no more learning about Islam unless it was from him!

When I look back on this, I have often wondered what her husband might have been aware of while living in the Muslim culture of Morocco before 9-11. (Jackie had called me that day when I was home recovering, asking what I knew about the whole event because she knew I kept up a little more on the news then she did.)

Sometime later I moved to a different city, and we lost contact. I still wonder if her husband might have been fearful of their son becoming radicalized. I don't think anyone realized at that time that even Mosques in this country were being used to recruit American Muslims to join Al Qaeda or at least support them.

One thing all false religions and cults have in common is the ability to mix just enough truth to appear legitimate and attract a following. In the case of Islam, as I stated before, their 'Bible' is full of selected Old Testament content interspersed with Mohammed's version of God's word. Mohammed himself was no Jesus. His favorite wife was a 6-year-old girl that he at least waited until she was 9 to have intercourse with. His hatred of Jews runs all the way through the Quran and *Allah* is a vengeful, unforgiving, convert-by-the-sword, unapproachable deity. Mohammed never healed anyone or performed anything supernatural. He was a ruthless, spiritual dictator who said he believed Jesus was a prophet while practicing nothing taught by Christ! He never added anything from the teachings of Christ to the Quran. There is also no such thing as forgiveness in Islam!

The only hope for Heaven is if you strictly follow every rule in the Quran. It also teaches that humans are born *good* and only do wrong because of outer influences; hence the covering of females to prevent men from lusting or raping (and the hypocrisy of this belief is obvious). It forbids music and books or movies that might contradict the Islamic creed and cause a 'good' Muslim to do evil. There is no comparison to Christianity on any level. There is no concept of free will in Islam, no teaching that women are equal to men in the eyes of their 'god', Allah. Mohammed never sacrificed anything, was never tortured, never offered a single new spiritual truth, and died a natural death without any evidence of a resurrection.

Anyone with the slightest knowledge of Islam knows that believing that it is a 'Religion of Peace' is laughable. There is nothing peaceful about killing people because they refuse to become a Muslim. This false and dangerous religion should have never risen to the height of being called one of the three greatest religions in the world! The fact that Islam dominates most of Middle

East culture is the reason they have remained incompatible with western (and Christian) values and continue to exist as only Third-World nations.

I am aware that many Muslims are good, peaceful people... They are not the problem! We cannot call ourselves Christian if we blame all Muslims for the damage caused by the bad actors in that faith. I *do* believe it is important to know the truth behind the mindset that resulted in 9-11 and all the other conflicts and misery this religion has caused. Muslim leaders plan to continue these conflicts until they achieve their goal of world dominance. It would be wise to remember that this battle for truth has been going on since the birth of Ishmael, recorded in the Old Testament! It is also helpful to remember that there is good and there is evil, and evil beliefs always result in devastation, misery, and death.

America and all nations that recognize the rights of every citizen to live free from tyranny and elect their leaders evolved *only* from Christian teachings! The right to life, liberty and the pursuit of happiness as stated in our Constitution are the 'Inalienable rights from *God*'.

Another common denominator of a false religion is the hypocrisy that eventually reveals it. Mohammed lived a debased life but held himself up as a true prophet of God! Jim Jones is another example of a false prophet who led hundreds of foolish believers to drink his poisoned 'Kool-Aid' in the compound he created for his Utopia in Guyana. Because of their spiritual needs and ignorance, he had convinced hundreds that he would provide a perfect environment where they would be safe with him as their 'Messiah' and, of course, would honor him with all their worldly possessions! Knowing how to discern truth is the greatest protection we can have in this life. There are many people in this world who long for a spiritual leader but have ignored all the warning signs the Bible gives in order to avoid falling for false prophets. Jesus warned that *many would come claiming to be the Christ*, and history is full of them. Even here in America too many tend to worship ordinary humans, such as political leaders, as if they can create a perfect, equally good outcome for everyone. To hold up *any* human, including a Pope or a Pastor, as infallible is what the Bible calls '*idol worship*' and will never produce the results expected.

Faith and Discernment:

What is totally embarrassing is the number of Christians who fall for these false prophets! I am now recalling my own experience after leaving my abusive marriage in California. When I was living there, I attended a small church (mainly because it gave me a break from the jerk I was married to). I eventually became friends with a very fun lady, Bonnie, who was a member there, and we started to socialize a lot. She knew the Bible like no one I had met before, and we would talk for hours and share a lot of our personal lives. She was also married and had a child the same age as mine. My own Christianity was so lame; I totally trusted her take on it.

It was about a year later that I finally had enough abuse, got divorced and moved back to my home state of Washington. I started my own business, and after about a year or so, Bonnie contacted me. I was surprised to hear that she was divorced and wanting to move, hoping she could find a job and resume our friendship. It was 1988, and after she arrived, she wanted to share her belief that the *'Rapture'* was about to happen.

*The 'Rapture' is the common way most Christians refer to the return of Christ for His church. This is *not* His second coming to Earth, but the 'catching up' of believers (living and dead) before God's wrath against the Antichrist begins. This world-shaking, supernatural event will happen before, or perhaps during, the seven years of the Antichrist's rule. Jesus said to *be watchful and ready for this event*! (More on this subject in another chapter, but 1st Thessalonians 4:16-17 is a good place to start if interested.)

Bonnie also wanted me to read her copy of a book by Edgar Whisenant titled *88 Reasons Why the Rapture Will Be in 1988_*...sometime around September. 11th to the 13th. I read it, and being Biblically ignorant, I thought it was believable. The next time we met, she said she wanted me to share a motel room on the 13th of September if it hadn't happened before then. Wanting to be raptured myself, I agreed!

I think that night we had some prayer time before going to sleep in the divided bedrooms. Morning arrived, and I called out for Bonnie. When I went to her room, I saw the bed perfectly made and no sign of her! "Crap!" I said out loud, horrified I had been LEFT BEHIND! But soon the door opened and there was Bonnie with a cup of coffee and a newspaper.

It was not much longer before Bonnie's odd views of Christianity became more obvious, and she returned to California after our friendship dissolved.

As I mentioned before, my Bible knowledge was pathetic until after 9-11-2001. If I had just talked with a genuine Bible student instead of Bonnie, I would have been aware that her Bible-smarts were not all that! Sometime later I did read the passages myself where Jesus says, *"No one will know the day or the hour, not even the Son, but only the Father"* (Matthew 25:6, paraphrased, and many more places in scripture). Edgar was just one of many false prophets who have predicted a day or year that this would take place. All of them are guilty of the egregious sin of misusing God's word. Many have also misinterpreted the word *'quickly'* when Christ spoke of His return, believing He meant soon. Even the Disciples thought He would return in their lifetime. The original Greek word appearing in English as 'quickly' when translated properly is 'unexpectedly'. This is evidenced by His follow-up statement: *'like a thief in the night'*.

There are so many I have encountered who are almost as ignorant of the Bible and Christianity as I used to be, and I am still no Bible scholar myself. I just hope God still looks at me as a work-in-progress! I have often wondered about Bonnie and hoped she had a real 'Come-to-Jesus' moment. She was so sure of her understanding of scripture and had even led Bible classes in that church! The Bible says even Christians will have to defend their actions before God. This is called the *'Bema Seat' or Judgment Seat* of Christ. (2nd Corinthians 5: 10, and other scriptures). We cannot lose our salvation, but we will have to admit and acknowledge our failings after accepting Christ. (I'm thinking these will be the failings we have not *already* repented for or are just not even aware of.) Well, I am still comforted by knowing that His justice is perfect, and every consequence will be perfectly justified. I now know that if we claim to be a follower of Christ, it's going to be important that we handle His word with great care and discernment!

Chapter 8
HYPOCRISY and MISCONCEPTIONS

The reason Jesus was able to save the adulteress from being stoned to death was because he pointed out the hypocrisy of the accusers. Scripture says Jesus had been brought to the woman by the men to see if He would follow the edicts of the religious custom to have her stoned to death. It says Jesus began writing in the sand until all the men walked away. When He asked the woman *'Who is condemning you?'* she answered that *'no one was because they had all left'*. This is when Jesus told her that He also did not condemn her, but told her to *'go and sin no more'* (John 8:11). Many have tried to imagine what it was that Jesus wrote in the sand that caused her accusers to leave, but it is agreed by most Bible scholars that he wrote something that exposed their hypocrisy. (The 'sand message' is something I would like to ask him about someday!)

Hypocrisy knows no race or culture because everyone but Jesus is likely guilty of it. If you take the time to do any Bible study, it will be quickly obvious that hypocrisy was probably the most prevalent sin that he condemned in his ministry while on earth. He called the religious leaders of that time hypocrites because they heaped all kinds of restrictions on the people while ignoring them for themselves. This is the base of Jesus' admonition against judging others, and it was not meant as the 'woke' culture thinks it is! They think when He told His followers not to judge others it meant we should always be tolerant and accepting of human faults, including immorality. They often refer to the scripture in Matthew 7:1-5 that, paraphrased, says *we are not to judge so that we will not be judged.* Taken out of context and without study of related scripture, it is easy to see why it has been interpreted that way. In 1st John 5:1, Jesus calls a man a hypocrite for judging a 'brother' (fellow believer) and tells him that *he needs to take the log out of his own eye so he can see clearly enough to take the speck of sawdust out of his brothers.* In other words, Jesus was trying to make him aware that we have no right to judge another if we ourselves are guilty of similar sin. He warned that our *'judgment'* is to be without hypocrisy, or we will be judged in the same manner. (I also think this means we would be judged by others in *this* life as well as later by God.) Meanwhile today, the hypocritical 'woke' crowd feels completely free to judge and even punish anyone who disagrees with their spiritual or political ideology.

Here and now in our society, I see hypocrisy rampant in every area of life. It permeates religion, politics, and every institution we can observe! It can be seen in our personal lives as well. For instance, the whole COVID-19 lockdown enforcement was imposed on the masses, but not on most of the folks imposing it on others! Here in my state, the governor stopped all construction work unless it was construction on a *government* project! Most construction workers are safety-instructed, wearing protective gear like masks and gloves in their jobs, and usually work more than the required six feet apart on the site anyway! Totally hypocritical! So many lives harmed by this arbitrary shutting down of businesses without any reason or consideration of the workers or financial cost! Apartment construction was stopped as well as residential homes. Many who were waiting to occupy them had to find other housing. Businesses who were trying to finish construction were out of luck, and so were the employees who needed the jobs! The well-paid officials, claiming to 'follow the science' when the science did not support their actions at all, could not have cared less. People were kept from attending a church service, having a wedding, or going to a restaurant even if they followed all the required protocol while countless rioting and violence in the streets was allowed without consequences! Pure, blatant hypocrisy!

Even in our own families, most of us can remember a time when we caught our parents being hypocritical. This would usually be a time when we were being punished for something a sibling had gotten away with. We usually expressed our feelings of justifiable outrage by yelling "NOT FAIR!" Well, we have every right to call out the unfairness of hypocrisy in our leaders as well.

The damage caused by the sin of hypocrisy is vast. Right now, in February of 2021, our own Congress is engaging in their on-going hypocrisy with a second impeachment of a duly elected president. This is even happening after he has left office! They have accused him of inciting an insurrection against the government on January 6th. The claim by the biased liberal Democrats, including our mainstream media, was that during a speech that day he encouraged and expected his supporters to riot, attack the Capitol and stop the transfer of power to the newly elected president, Joe Biden. Nothing in that speech was a call for an 'insurrection' or even for a riot. Much more will be known about this as time reveals, but President Trump, flawed as he is, was rightly found not guilty (again)!   I believe this was not only because of the actual wording used in the speech but also because the hypocrisy of the accusers was revealed. So, just like the men who accused the woman caught in adultery, they also had to 'walk away'.

Hypocrisy of Anti-Capitalism:

Another memory of my time working at the safe house was a meeting we had discussing our feelings regarding wealthy people. I was not surprised at the comments from the staff considering that they all had graduated from the very 'woke' Evergreen College, here in Washington (where every student is expected to be a committed socialist).

The discussion leader asked us to say how we would feel in a social setting with rich people. Since every staff member was from an upper-income family, their answers would probably perplex most people. One young staffer said she would feel extremely uncomfortable and too intimidated to engage with any of them. Another said they would feel anxious and would want to leave as soon as possible. All said they would feel completely out of place and unable to relate!

When it came my turn, I asked how many of them realized that it was only wealthy people who made their jobs possible, providing the funds to operate this non-profit agency we worked in. (They just stared at each other blankly in response.)

I also offered my own reactions to being in the company of wealthy people. I told them I would politely approach them and ask some questions like; where they were from and what did they do to become successful? I would ask them about their families and interests. I would certainly thank them for their generosity in giving financial support to important causes, like our agency! I would also ask them what their biggest concerns were and what their worst challenges were and how they overcame them. I concluded by telling the staff I would look at it as almost equal to taking an advanced class in business economics while making some possible contacts for my future!

I got a lot of deer-in-the-headlights expressions but at least a favorable response from the discussion leader. I'm sure being much older than the staff was a factor, but I do believe I had also been blessed by a family who taught me to never feel inferior to, or resentful of, those with wealth. I was assured by them that rich people had problems and family issues just like anyone else. The old saying that *'Rich folks put their pants on one leg at a time just like poor folks'* is a truth to remember as well.

I did not want to add to their discomfort by pointing out the hypocrisy of their 'feelings' as I think I caused enough culture-shock already. I could have told them the story of killing the goose that laid the golden egg, but they probably wouldn't see the point of it anyway. That story is a perfect lesson about not appreciating (or protecting) the source that produced the 'gold'. The goose was killed because of ignorance and greed, but the allegory applies to the fact that anti-capitalists can also be guilty of 'killing' the source of prosperity we are blessed with in America. It is a terrible shame that we have allowed this movement to gain so much traction in the past few decades! I also know these anti-capitalists were never told the truth about socialism and what it does to destroy the countries that operate under it. If you ask them, they will always try to claim that there is *good* socialism in countries like Sweden, which is not exactly a socialist government. It is very capitalistic with their economy, except for a much higher tax rate to cover their social programs. The real lesson would be to observe what happened to Venezuela.

I won't include a history lesson on Venezuela because the info is easily available. The point is that not too long ago Venezuela had become one of the most prosperous, self-supporting, desirable countries in the world. Somehow the socialists were able to take control and their anti-capitalist policies have turned that country into another Third-World nation. There are rampant food shortages and the people have lost their freedom and hope under the current dictatorship. If Americans do not stay vigilant, it could happen here. The truth is Socialism is just Communism-light and will only produce misery for everyone except the leadership.

Jesus Was Not a Socialist:

One of many biblical misconceptions, that even some Christians believe, is that Jesus was a 'liberal who would support a socialist government. I once had a conversation with a co-worker who made this claim. He was a fan of the current move to socialism in the Democrat Party and claimed to be a Christian. I told him about Jesus telling His followers that *if someone does not work, they should not eat.* The poor man was in his fifties, and his face turned quite red. He almost screamed at me that I was lying because Jesus would *never* have said such a thing! Since I was at my computer, and Google *can* be a friend, I quickly found the scripture (2ⁿᵈ Thessalonians 3:10) and read it to him. He was still almost hyperventilating when he said, "Well, that's not how *you* said it!" He then abruptly left to continue his work or something, and he generally avoided me after that.

This is another thing I have observed about liberals. They always refuse to continue any discussion that includes an opinion or information they don't like. They really are unwilling, or maybe just unprepared, to have a respectful debate. Personally, I appreciate getting any information that might change my mind about an issue. I find it hard to understand why someone would not want to find out that their opinion might be unfounded!

I am beginning to not be surprised by the hysterical reactions from the 'woke' crowd who get so upset when their beliefs are challenged! I'm sure I would get the same reaction from that man if I were to include the scripture from 1ˢᵗ Timothy 5:8 that says *relatives* are supposed *to* provide for their own in need. In other words, Jesus was not in favor of making the taxpayers (or government) responsible for them! Sadly, ignorant atheists and non-Christians often claim that those scriptures are proof of how 'wrong and uncaring' Christianity is. They ignore the fact that Jesus clearly instructs us to share with those who are disabled or mentally ill and without a family or friends to help them.

My own father, as wonderful as he was, believed many misconceptions about God and Christianity. (Earlier in this book, I mentioned there were some issues with my father that would surface.) A puzzling thing I found out about him when I was an adult was that even though he was adamant about politics and world events, he never voted! When I asked him why, he just said, "Because it never makes any difference." I also found out that when he was in high school during the '30s, he was a member of the *Young Communist Club*. Yes, it existed then. He was one of several students that loved the idea of a 'benevolent dictator' who would make sure everyone was equal and there was no poverty or crime because everyone would share all they had, and no one would be without. (Sounds a lot like the '60s 'All-we-need-is-love' folks and a certain political party today!) My dad had a loving heart, but I never agreed with all of his thinking.

My dad owned the small house we had lived in and later rented out. A few renters came and went until a family with three boys moved in. They were very good renters, taking care of the landscaping and fixing anything the property required. My dad would always buy anything they needed for the upkeep and would forgive some of the rent in exchange for their labor. All very admirable, and I respected him for that, but after some years had passed, I found out that he never raised the rent! I remember the time the renters insisted that they pay at least $300 a month and how my dad protested, but reluctantly accepted. This was in the '90s when rents were at least $600 or more for a three-bedroom home! I finally asked him why he did not charge what he could, and he answered with, "How could they afford to take care of the boys if I raised the rent?" He also said he was happy to have people take care of the home and enough rental income to cover the property taxes. Some years later, they bought a very nice RV home and moved out of state after their boys were raised. If only every so-called 'woke' liberal/progressive/socialist was as good with their activism as my dad! In their political Utopia, only the government would own property, but the elite would live where and how they pleased!

My dad was almost an atheist, but mostly an agnostic. When I was in my forties and beyond, before he passed away, we would have many talks about spiritual matters, politics and world events. His favorite comeback to anything biblical was: "If God was so good, why does He allow all the bad in the world?" No amount of explaining to my dad that aside from natural disasters and most accidents, every act of evil is because of human free will. (Come to think of it, why would we need free will if God intervened and made everything safe, perfect and wonderful?)

Having free will is part of what makes us humans created 'in the image of God'. God even gave his angels free will just as He has free will to do all that He does. God did not want robots, He wanted humans to love and revere Him by choice. Well, my dad never gave up his view that God should intervene whenever anything harmful was about to happen. I even appealed to his common dad-sense by asking how a child could be expected to *learn* if the parent always stepped in to prevent them from making a mistake, getting hurt or causing harm to themselves or others? How would anyone learn the difference between right and wrong? Jesus said to think of God the Father as *'Abba'* (the

Aramaic name for daddy), and I tried to get my dad to see things from that perspective as well.

It is obvious that loving children requires discipline, teaching and providing rewards or consequences as needed. Also, a *loving* parent does not automatically take their child's side until they know the facts. For instance, whenever I would come crying to my dad about being bullied or mistreated, the first thing he did was to ask me what I had done! After I got through tearfully explaining what had happened prior to my trauma, he would point out what part I had played in the whole event. I learned at a young age that I'd better do some introspection before expecting any sympathy!

This life lesson compares to the story of Adam and Eve in the garden after they had been disobedient by eating the forbidden fruit. Paraphrasing here: The 'Father' asked Eve why she disobeyed. She answered that *the Serpent had told her it would all be good, and she would not suffer any consequences, but would be like God, knowing good from evil and not die as God had warned.* When God asked Adam about eating the fruit, he answered: *'That woman you gave me; she offered it to me!'* (Nice going, Adam! Just toss Eve under the bus as well as trying to put it back on God.) Read Genesis, chapter 3 for the whole sorry story.

The point of the event in the garden was that God wanted them to know what part they played in choosing to disobey. As a loving Father, He also could not let it 'slide' and therefore allowed them to experience the consequences. God had provided them with a perfect environment, and, as far as I'm concerned, Adam deserved the worst of the consequences for being such a wimp and a jerk!

Since my dad was so much like this Father-God who called out the disobedience of the first two humans, as well as being an honest, loving, morally upright man, I was perpetually confused about his reluctance to believe! I can only conclude that his thinking was based on the Communist teaching that humans can create a perfect society without God's help or any religious beliefs, but with the right dictator of course! Unfortunately, that thinking has only continued to grow like a cancer since the '60s and is the basic reason for the political and social damage we are seeing today.

Another perplexing thing about my dad was that he was raised by Christian parents! Perhaps they should have attended a non-Mennonite church and include their children as well. As I mentioned earlier, they did not preach about their faith and were likely anti-church because of their Mennonite experience. Many of my dad's brothers were not churchgoers either, and his only sister became a Christian scientist and eventually a 'New-Age' believer. I must have been blessed to have Sally along with my grandparents' influence to direct my path! I was blessed that my dad was perfectly fine with all my church involvement, and he never talked despairingly about anyone who went to church.

An interesting question I would like to ask those who reject the Bible, including the very *existence* of Jesus, is whether or not they understand why our years are numbered as they are! I wonder how many would respond to the fact that it is currently 2022 because it has been two thousand and twenty-two years since the death and resurrection of Jesus! If He was just an ordinary man who was delusional in His claims, or a complete myth, why did the entire world accept the calendar starting over with the year of His death being year one?

I can guarantee you that there will be no calendar starting over when I die! No other human in history has been honored in this way! I can only surmise the 'woke' folks are not aware of this as there would surely be some demonstrations, riots and demands that the government correct this *'non-inclusive'* and, no doubt, *'racist'* decision! They would also have to protest all the scientific research that labeled historical time periods and discoveries as occurring in BC or AD (Before Christ or After Death). I think these terms have been recently renamed in some way, but I will have to research that myself. Even if revised, the significance of the calendar change cannot be denied.

Not Peace but a Sword:

Another misconception about Christianity is that Jesus was a unifying, gentle, always-forgiving Son of God who accepted all who claimed to believe in God and tried to live a good life. Many Christmas cards have the message from the angels announcing the birth of Christ saying, *'Peace on Earth, goodwill towards men.'* This is not an accurate quote. The original Greek as translated in the Bible is *'Peace on Earth to men of goodwill'* or *'to men on whom His favor rests'* (Luke 2:14). I saw a perfect example of this being correctly understood after 9-11. It was an article with a photo of two soldiers standing in front of a fighter-jet preparing to leave for Iraq. It was close to Christmas, and someone had painted the following on the side of the jet: *"Peace on Earth to men of goodwill...all others stand by!"* (I so wish I had clipped and saved that article!)

In Matthew 10:34-36 and Luke 12:49-53, we can read Jesus' claim that He *'did not come to bring peace, but a sword'*. He also said He came to *'bring fire on the Earth'* and how He *'wished it were already kindled'*, then added *'but I have a baptism to go through'*. He also said He *'came to bring division that would turn mothers against daughters, sons against fathers… and that a man's enemies would be from his own house'*. (Sounds awfully warm and woke, doesn't it?)

Of course, the 'sword' was the *truth of God's word*, and according to scripture Jesus is the *'word that became flesh and dwelt among men'* (John 1:1 and 14 paraphrased).

Jesus also wasn't very meek and gentle when he made a whip and started knocking over the tables full of items for sale in the courtyard of the Holy Temple in Jerusalem! Talk about judgmental! He also frequently riled up the religious leaders by repeatedly calling them *'snakes'* and a *'nest of vipers'* (Matthew 23:33). This side of Jesus was shown when it was *righteously* required. He pointed out their hypocrisy in the strongest terms because of the way they treated the people they were claiming to teach spiritual truth to. In our world today, His reactions and manner of speaking would be considered rude or too judgmental, as this is not the loving, compassionate Jesus many imagine Him exclusively to be. This is why it is important to understand the whole truth about the character and purpose of God and His Holy word.

Another scripture many fail to understand is the one where Jesus declares that if people *'love mother, father, sons or daughters more than Me, they are not worthy of Me'* (Matthew 10:37 paraphrased). In my opinion, there is nothing clearer about what He meant than when I read or hear about a crime committed by a kid and the family declares that it could not be their child! Many will outright lie to protect them. Some will go so far as to hide them or help them escape the law or any kind of consequences! Watch any news broadcast when they interview families about a relative or friend (who even has a criminal record), making every excuse they can come up with! I see it every day in the news as well as on a smaller scale in families that lie about or enable bad behavior.

I found that this scripture also makes sense if you substitute the word 'Me' with 'righteousness'. If someone claims to love Christ (righteousness) but puts their love for their child (spouse, friend, relative, Pastor or political leader) above what is *right*, why wouldn't Jesus reject them? Jesus exemplifies God's righteousness, so I think looking at His teaching this way negates any perceived harshness in Jesus' words. Many also seem to think that Christ would excuse the denials or cover-ups of wrong behavior as simply proof of *loyalty* or 'love' for the guilty person, especially if it is a family member. This attitude also goes against the teaching of Christ that we are to love the sinner but hate the sin! The wrong-doer deserves the consequence, and trying to prevent the consequence is not loving the wrong-doer and not loving Christ *or* what is right! (And loyalty is not always proof of 'love'.)

A perfect example of this just occurred in Minnesota as I am writing this in April 2021. A young man named Daunte Wright was pulled over by police for driving with expired tabs. His plates were run, and they saw he had a warrant for his arrest for skipping a court date regarding armed robbery and illegal possession of a firearm. He was 19 years old. Before the police approached the car, he called his mom and said he was pulled over because he had air fresheners hanging from the visor. When he was standing outside the car door about to be handcuffed, he decided to jump back in the car to take off. Another officer pulled what she thought was her taser and yelled "Taser" three times as required to alert anyone near to avoid the voltage. Sadly, for still unknown reasons, it was her *gun*, not a taser, and she tragically realized she had shot him. He still drove away but crashed and was pronounced dead from the gunshot. As soon as his mother was contacted, she said the police used the air freshener excuse to justify pulling him over… because he is black. She later went on to say he had the mentality of a 17-year-old because she had 'babied' him so much, but added 'he was a sweet, well-liked young man who did not deserve to die'. I don't recall anyone saying he "deserved to die"! (His family had also lost the $10,000.00 they paid to get him out of jail due to the $100,000.00 bail because he did not show up in court for his previous crime! And this usually means they are required to pay the additional $90,000.00 owed.)

A whole lot of wrong-sauce going on here! Of course, he did not deserve to die, and the tragedy of the officer's mistake resulted in her being charged now with manslaughter, even though the usual mobs, like Black Lives Matter protestors, are calling it 'another murder of a young black male'. Riots, destruction, and looting began just hours after the incident, and Daunte is being hailed as another 'innocent victim of police racism'. To make matters worse, the media and many political leaders are declaring that the white female officer *meant* to kill Daunte because of his race! I was asked once what I would do if my own child was accused of a crime. Like my dad, I would first want to know the truth! But if they were guilty, wouldn't I want to keep my own child from prison? Of course I would want to.

It is human nature to want nothing to hurt your child! But this is what is meant by the need for 'tough love'. Keeping anyone from facing the consequences of their actions is *not* 'loving' them! There are countless news stories about parents who refuse to believe or admit their child was so out of control at school that police had to intervene. Even when a video proves what the child was doing!

This is another sad result of the child-rearing fads that were accepted since the '60s when people were told that they needed to be a 'friend' to their child instead of a parent. The book of Proverbs in the Old Testament has hundreds of child-rearing tips that if followed would produce happier children who would become much better, well-adjusted adults! Loving anyone should never mean overlooking or excusing their wrong actions, choices, or attitudes. The essence of Jesus' admonition to not love even your own family more than Him, might be further understood by the scriptures in Hebrews 12:6 and Revelations 3:19; *'The Lord chastens those He loves'* and *'Those I love, I rebuke and discipline'*.

If what I have written on this subject has given anyone the impression that I must be the kind of mother who would never raise a problem child, I will explain why I still refer to my daughter as my 'Prodigal Child' in another chapter.

Jesus Was Not a Pacifist:

This is another false belief about Christ that persists with some denominations and many Christian believers. My own grandparents left Germany to avoid the mandatory military service that was against the Mennonite church doctrine. The Quakers are another sect that teaches against participating in wars because they believe God would not condone it. I have known some Christians who claim that Jesus would never do anything but *'turn the other cheek'* even in threatening circumstances! Sigh…this is what comes from a limited study of scripture.

A man once argued with me that Jesus never told His disciples to use a weapon. He cited the scene during the arrest of Christ in the garden of Gethsemane when Peter used his sword to cut off the ear of one of the soldiers.

Jesus rebuked him and restored the soldier's ear. In Matthew 26:52, Jesus also tells them (paraphrased), *'He who lives by the sword shall die by the sword.'* What this man missed was the meaning of *'lives by'*. Jesus was saying that we should never be the *aggressor.* He was warning His followers that if we instigate violence, we will eventually bring that on ourselves. He was not saying we should not be prepared to defend ourselves or others against an attack. Peter was wrong because the soldiers were not trying to *kill* Jesus in the garden; they were only there to arrest him.

I further went on to prove my point by showing this man the scripture where Jesus tells His disciples to *'sell their cloaks and purchase swords'*. This was during the Last Supper described in Luke 22:36 because He wanted them to be armed against the threats and violent attacks He knew would come from their enemies after His death and resurrection.

A Misunderstood Commandment:

"Thou shalt not take the name of the Lord your God in vain" (Genesis 20:7). I remember hearing a radio minister regarding this third commandment who offered an interpretation that clarified its meaning. I had always thought this commandment *had* to refer to something far more serious than using His name to crudely swear or cuss! He explained that the true meaning is found in the Hebrew translation of the word *'take'*. According to the original Hebrew that word translates to *bear, carry or lift up.* Some Bible versions use, *'Do not take up the name.'* The NIV Bible says, *'misuse the name'*. This minister went on to add that during ancient times Pagans put the names of their 'gods' on banners or other objects that were carried, displayed, and taken into battles or conquest missions in order to justify their actions. (I found a lot of additional information confirming this view when I 'Google searched' my question about this.)

My personal view of *'carrying His name'* can pertain to wearing a cross or putting a Christian symbol on your car bumper. When you drive like a jerk with a symbol like that on your car you have just *'taken' the Lord's name in vain*! When people wear a cross, but act in an un-Christian way, they are also *'taking'* His name in vain.

What I do not believe is meant by 'taking the Lord's name in vain' is when I express some righteous outrage by calling out, "Jesus Christ!" I am comfortable answering the response of "You're taking His name in vain!" with "No, it is *not* in vain, it's a plea!" (It still results in some pearl-clutching, but I suppose I'll find out if it offends Him when my time comes.)

It is a very serious commandment and I see it constantly misused! Every time a false prophet or preacher uses His Holy name to justify their unearned wealth, or a politician claims their words or actions are on 'God's side' when they pass a new law that hurts or misleads their constituents, it is a *misuse!* It is also shameful that we need to be suspicious of a business that has a Christian symbol on their website or advertising because of some who claim to be Christian while acting nothing like it in practice!

In Islam God's name is always used to justify and even celebrate their terrorist attacks! They also claim their cultural practices, no matter how barbaric, are done in 'God's name'! Christians do not accept that Allah is the same God as Jehovah, but the misuse is still obvious.

Scripture adds that the misuse of the name of God may not be forgiven when it is directly used to *'blaspheme the Holy Spirit'* (Deuteronomy 5:11). An important commandment indeed!

I am far from a Bible scholar, but I am hoping some of what I have shared is acceptable to Him. I pray for continued help from this *'comforter'* (the third part of the Holy Trinity of God) that Jesus promised to send when we accepted Him as our Savior. Jesus said the Holy Spirit would help us understand the truth of His word and His will for our lives! (John 14: 16-18 and 26). This same spirit also takes our most awkwardly presented prayers and makes them acceptable to the Father. Scripture also says we can *'grieve'* the Holy Spirit by ignoring His presence and help in our lives! (Ephesians 4:30, and *many* others.)

For years my most frequent prayer was for God not to give up on me, and I now believe that this answered prayer was because the Holy Spirit was likely pleading for this grace on my behalf!

Chapter 9
CHOICES and CONSEQUENCES

Well, the truth is that even though I was blessed by my immigrant grandparents with their Christian values, and accepted Christ as a teen, I veered far from those teachings for too many years.

I am guilty of failing my own child due to my reluctance to make her face the consequences of her behavior on too many occasions. My first mistake was assuming she was just a carbon copy of me who would never think to do anything to bring dishonor on me, just as I never would have done anything to dishonor my family in a major way.

As an adult, I also assumed the high school 'sweetheart' that I married was as determined as I was to be a dedicated spouse, and the best parent a child could have. Although this man had many attractive qualities, he was not that interested in being a parent, or even a faithful husband. I, in turn, believed I could win him over if I just started to go along with his party-lifestyle choices.

I also naïvely believed that our daughter would be okay despite all this. I learned the hard way that neglect is not just physical. Neglect can be more than abusively punishing a child, depriving them of food, inflicting emotional abuse or withholding affection. If anything, Claire had more privileges and indulgences that were actually *not* good for her! Indulging her because of our guilt from indulging our own desires proved to be another example of 'loving' a child more than we loved Christ and His righteousness.

This kind of poor parenting may not be seen as bad as in the case of the young man and others who wind up in prison or dead due to the scape-goating and indulgence from their families, but it is still one side of the same coin. In my case, the real problems with my daughter did not become obvious until she started tenth grade.

After my divorce from that short but abusive second marriage, I moved back to Washington with Claire and started my own business. I was working more than twelve hours a day and Claire was attending a local high school. I assumed (again) that she cared as much about my needs as I cared about my dad's when he was raising me and my brothers. (Assumptions are not very wise

I have learned). I also assumed she was doing okay in school. I did not know what she was up to until I saw her report card that first semester. She was failing all her classes! I then discovered that she never went to class after showing up for first period and never did any homework! She was always home when I got off work at 6:30, and she would always assure me her homework was done and I never questioned it.

Well, a destructive pattern became obvious. I'm going to call it my 'trust but verify' flaw. In fact, this could occupy a whole chapter by itself! But I will leave that for later.

I soon found out that my daughter had met up with other teens that also just skipped school! They hopped on a city bus and spent all day hanging out at the Seattle Center. When I asked the school why I was never contacted about her attendance, they said it was their policy to take attendance in first period only and after that considered the student to be there for the day!

This was in the mid-'80s, but today they take attendance for each class, possibly because the 'Becca Bill' was passed in 1996 in response to a deadly attendance and truancy issue. This bill was named for a young girl named Becca who was murdered while she was skipping school and her parents had not been kept informed about her truancy. Today every parent in my state can go online if they choose to see if their child was in class or not. The school can threaten to implement the Becca Bill if a student reaches the limit on missing school without an excuse, even if it is just certain classes. This means if the truancy persists the parent will have to go to court to plead their case. If the judicial decision favors the parent but the criteria are not followed, the student will be placed in juvenile detention, or the parent will face jail time themselves!

After finding out about Claire's truancy, I called her dad and told him what was going on. To my surprise, even though he was remarried and working long hours, he promised to help by talking to her and even driving her to school every morning. This seemed to be helping for a while, but she eventually went back to skipping school. I was the only provider with a small amount of child support until she turned 18, and it was a real struggle just to pay for rent the first few years of my business. I now know that her self-esteem was so low that she was only happy getting the attention she craved from the crowd she chose to be with. I also was pathetically naïve about what the Seattle Center had become by the mid-eighties!

The Seattle Center I remembered was just a fun and interesting place with rides, games and a big food court, plus a science center and other exhibits that kids could go to on weekends or with a class field trip. I was shocked to find out it was now infested with gangs and other 'feral' kids that hung out all day and looked for trouble as well. I started getting phone calls from young men looking for my daughter. Some could barely speak proper English and would say a lot of threatening things. I once stayed up all night by the front door after calling the police because one of them said he was on his way with a gun to our apartment. I sat there with a baseball bat and a knife even though the police said they were very close by and could be there in less than a minute if I called! Fortunately, the thug never showed up. I had made Claire stay in her room with a girlfriend while I kept watch that night. Things were not going well to say the least.

Her father and I decided to get her into counseling (as a family) to try and turn things around. Unfortunately, neither of us, nor the counselor, could compete with Claire's strong will to go her own way. I was not a mature enough Christian to do what was needed and could not undo what had contributed to her choices. I do believe that a strong-willed child like my daughter might have made better choices if there had also been a dedicated dad in our home.

Even so, I had also neglected the Christian responsibility to make sure she knew about God and what the Bible teaches about life choices. But despite my Christian background, I was still too ignorant of God's word and too reliant on my own 'wisdom'.

Eventually she served several short jail times for shoplifting and other misdemeanors. (Oddly she was never guilty of a felony.) I did post bail for a few situations, but she always showed up for court and always promised to reform. Her crimes were usually for a $40 theft in order to get a motel for the night. (Even though she preferred to be homeless, she wanted to clean up occasionally and sleep in a bed.) I continued to hope she would tire of this, but after another two years of not even knowing where she was, I decided to tell myself that she had died so I could deal with life and supporting myself. This was an extreme embarrassment within my family as my daughter was the only person (that I knew of) in our entire family to have ever been arrested, even going back to the late 1800s!

To make a very long story short, she eventually came around and stayed with me sporadically. But sadly, she often returned to the streets. Before too long she became pregnant, conceived with a man who soon went back to prison. The child was Sasha, my granddaughter, who became my responsibility for more than a year when Claire went back to the streets again. After Sasha's father got out of prison, Claire married him. He was a charming and clever career criminal who abused her for years until she finally decided she had enough. At that time, she asked if she and Sasha could move back in with me. She promised that she was completely done with that lifestyle and was ready to be responsible. Sasha was about 10 years old then, but because of her parents' chaotic lifestyle, she was only at second grade level in school.

My Prodigal Child:

The story of the *Prodigal Child* is found in Luke 15: 11-32. Jesus used it to illustrate to his followers the nature of God regarding His love and refusal to give up on one of His own. The story is about one of two brothers who asked his father for an early inheritance so he could leave and go his own way. This brother wanted to live a rebellious and self-indulgent life, never intending to return home. The father agreed but was deeply grieved and waited each day, searching the landscape, hoping to see his son returning. Eventually things went bad for this young man, compelling him to return. His father spotted him afar off and rushed out to meet him! This wayward son now pleaded to his father for work as his servant, tending the flocks if only he would be allowed! Much to the outrage of his brother, the father rejoiced and welcomed this prodigal son with a party for him and his friends, including a golden ring and a glorious new robe to wear! (The Bible version is much better than my brief attempt here.) However, I could relate to that father's joy in having a child return with such a change of heart.

Well, this time my 'prodigal child' was finally good for her word, and Sasha quickly got up to her grade level with the stability she was experiencing. Another reason I believed Claire's metamorphosis was real was when she told me she would not seek or allow any men in her life until Sasha was grown and on her own. This is something I wished I had done when I divorced Claire's dad! As I said previously, I am the farthest thing from being a 'good' Christian, but somehow God has still not abandoned me! And speaking of abandoned, that was the one thing I had vowed after my mother left: that I would *never* abandon any child of mine! Well, I never 'left' my child physically, but in looking back, I know that I abandoned her emotionally and, even worse, spiritually.

Not too long after they began living with me, I decided I needed to ask my daughter for forgiveness. I had already asked forgiveness from God through my Savior Jesus, but it was bearing down hard on me to take this next step. By the grace of God, she understood and tearfully accepted all the truth about everything I regretted since her childhood. She then asked me to forgive her for the stress and misery she had brought into my life as well. Truth does set us free, as Jesus promised.

Even though I had been blessed by my immigrant grandparents' values and was able to escape most of the damage from the '60s rebellion, I still fell very short of what I should have been as a parent. I only know I *never* wanted to be a single parent! It is rarely a beneficial outcome for children and a difficult thing to choose to be without a mate when you are young, believing you still 'deserve' to have a loving relationship.

I had also bought into the idea that if a parent was 'happy', their children will be happy as well. (*Sounded good on paper!*) I now know what we in this world call love and happiness is not nearly as fulfilling as God's prescription for true love and human relationships!

A Broken Picker:

During my second marriage, my daughter had a junior high school friend who told me her mom was getting married for the sixth time. I asked her why her mom had been married so many times, and she simply responded with "Her picker's broken!" I couldn't help but laugh and wondered how this child had come up with such an amusing but odd declaration!

After that brief marriage ended, I was encouraged to try again by a very dear cousin who was finally happily married after the first two failed. (She asserted the old 'third-time-is-the-charm' adage). I think I told her that another try would likely fail because my picker was broken. She laughed at my reply but did not push me to reconsider. I have since learned that my 'broken picker' was due to what I now believe was my trust and assumption problem. If I had been smart enough to follow President Regan's advice to "Trust but verify", I would not have married either one of the men I chose. I realize now just how often my trust was not warranted and my assumptions were just my desire to believe what I hoped was true.

I was raised by a dad who always believed the best about everyone, and I thought that was the right way to think about others as well. This turned out to be a major problem with raising my daughter…always wanting to believe she was truthful and doing her best, without verifying these assumptions. I had also assumed her father would stop being a party-animal after she was born because I wanted that to be the case, even though there was no evidence he wanted to change. Two years after our divorce, I began a relationship with the man who would be my second husband. I remembered him as the boy-next-door, so when my dad told me he had come up from California to visit his folks, I decided to stop by to say hello. I knew he had never married and that he had a crush on me when we were kids! He was one of six boys who came from what I also assumed was a normal, good family. We seemed to connect, and he asked me out for a date. Glen was smart, fun, and attractive. He had a well-paid, responsible job, and he had recently purchased a three-bedroom house! It all got serious more quickly than it should have, but I 'believed' this had to be part of God's plan for me to finally have a solid and happy relationship and a good dad for Claire who was then 11 years old.

After many long distant phone calls and another trip up from California, I told him we should get married. He was hesitant, but eventually agreed even though it was so soon after we had been reacquainted. Glen's family was very happy their now 40-year-old bachelor son was going to get married! They had known me as the girl-next-door since I was about 12 years old, so it was all good as far as they were concerned.

Things quickly came together for a wedding that would take place in just a few more months. It would be somewhat formal but nothing as huge and formal as my first one! I would also be selling my house and bringing Claire and one cat to California. I would be leaving a great job, my best friends, and my extended family as well, so 'busy and stressful' would be an understatement for the weeks that followed!

Red Flags, Assumptions and Trust:

Before the wedding, Glen and I were visiting with my dad in the kitchen and discussing various things. He was agreeing with my dad that going to movies, restaurants and other entertainment activities was not something he liked to spend money on. I, on the other hand, was in the habit of going out on the town with my friends and to the movies and concerts as well. I chimed in with a comment like, "Wow, what do you do for fun?" or something like that. Suddenly, with a surprising amount of irritation in his voice, he looked straight at me and said, "You need to know, I am not always a very nice person." Of course, I laughed this comment off as I would others before we married, because I assumed he really was a nice guy at heart.

I heard a psychologist recently say that when people tell you things about themselves it would be wise to believe them.

After we married, I soon faced the fact that he was not the man I hoped he was. Even so, I stayed with him much longer than I should have. I was too embarrassed to admit this mistake to my family and friends, and I still believed he might change if I became the kind of wife he expected me to be.

During that four-year marriage, I also discovered it was not just me (and eventually Claire) that he abused! One of his former co-workers told me he quit his job because of Glen's constant criticism, always putting him and others down at work. Apparently Glen was on good terms with his boss, or I would think he would have been fired! Seems my second husband was 'not always a very nice person' just as he had told me. Despite this, there were many 'good' times during those years, so I continued to believe his *good side* would prevail!

Unfortunately he only became more controlling and critical. It eventually escalated to shoving and slapping as well. He would sometimes blame his behavior on having too much to drink, however he was just as abusive when sober. Mostly he would justify his outbursts by claiming it was something I or Claire had said or done. He even insisted that Claire and I needed to see a counselor, and he would go with us so I would understand how wrong we were.

The counselor saw each of us separately, then when he was ending the session with me, he said there was nothing wrong with Claire or me, but he would not be able to help Glen. I never knew what he told Glen, but nothing changed.

I found myself starting to dread 5:30 every day when he came home from work. When I could no longer ignore this reality, it was a bitter pill to swallow. My hope of having a lasting relationship after the fourteen unhappy years of my first one was dead.

I now realize that not only had I ignored the many red flags that were waving around me, but I also left God out of all my decisions. To me, prayer was only part of a church service, not a regular part of my life. God was 'out there' somewhere, not within me as Jesus said He would be. Not a *'comforter'* in the form of a Holy Spirit I could ask for advice or share my thoughts with! Fortunately, by God's never-ending grace, I have come to understand another lesson from His word when Jesus said, *"Ye have not because ye ask not"* (James 4:2-3).

I have no regrets about my decision to become 'celibate' again and live my life without trying to find that perfect mate to share it with. The biggest regret for leaving at that time was because Claire had to leave the friends she had made in California, and I am sure that did not help her adjust to starting over at almost 15 in Seattle! I would advise any parent that, unless your children are used to moving, like is often necessary in military families, it can have a devastating effect on a teen. As I mentioned before, it was many years later that I needed to ask her forgiveness for that as well.

So much happened after leaving California! The details of having a business with fifteen employees for more than seven years, then taking other jobs and going through years of Claire's rebellion plus many other lessons God was trying to teach me would be like writing a book as lengthy as *War and Peace*! I am just grateful He never gave up on me and continues to teach me as He sees fit! My challenge, and prayer, is to be a good student.

Chapter 10
A TEACHABLE SPIRIT

An unexpected thing occurred sometime later after Claire came back to stay. One day she asked me why I kept reading the Bible so much. After leaving her abusive situation, we were beginning to bond again as a family. My daughter was aware that I did not attend a church then, but apparently was somewhat surprised to see me reading my Bible so often. She said, "Haven't you finished it yet? Why do you need to read it over and over?" Well, I think she caught me off- guard for a minute, but my answer came easily somehow. I told her that every time I read a section I had read before, something different was revealed! She seemed to find this odd but interesting, and we started to talk more about the Bible. She had been given a Bible when she was a child after attending a brief summer Bible school camp in our old neighborhood, but I had never insisted she study it.

It is not in my nature to push religion on anyone, just as my family never did when I was growing up. Claire was not ready to become a Bible student yet, but she started to read a mailer she ordered titled "Our Daily Bread", a Christian devotional booklet that arrived every month. Over the next few years, she would sometimes leave me a note for when I got home from work asking me about a certain Bible verse or subject she did not understand. We had developed a fun way to communicate with her calling me *Lucy.* Many of her written questions would start out with "Lucy! You got some 'splainin' to do!" before posing the question. She once told me I was her 'Bible'. I was, and am, humbled by this, but all I could do was answer if I could, but I also wanted to help her understand that much of scripture can be explained by other scripture...a daunting task for someone so new to the Bible. The biggest blessing here is that she had been gifted with a 'teachable spirit'!

I have recently been made aware of just how rare the gift of a teachable spirit is! I have decided that this is something I need to pray for my grandchildren as well as myself! When I look back on my interactions and debates with family, friends, or strangers, I realize how sadly this quality is missing in so many. A *teachable spirit* is present in anyone humble enough to know they don't know and are open to a different way of looking at a situation or subject. People with this quality are much more fun to be around! Those with a teachable spirit seem to be more curious about life in general and willing to learn. They are never boastful or arrogant and will never shut down others who disagree with them. (Hmmm…I'm thinking of the many liberal-thinking types I have encountered that seem to lack this quality almost without exception!)

I am remembering a co-worker that seemed to lack a teachable spirit. Another employee referred to him as a 'know-it-all' and I had many conversations with him that validated that opinion! The odd thing was he seemed to like that description because he smiled when he told me his wife gave him a coffee mug that had the message *"I don't need Google, my husband knows everything!"* He was also a committed Democrat liberal who believed every bit of racist, biased news and opinions from the left-leaning media, including the belief that human embryos are not babies! Another odd thing about him was how helpful he was whenever asked. He even did a few minor repairs for me when I mentioned a need. He explained that as a Mason it was his duty to be as helpful to others as possible to become what he called 'a man of God'. (I'm thinking this man would fit the definition of a *conundrum*.) Unfortunately, Masonic teachings are like many religious sects that mistakenly believe that 'good works' will earn the favor of God and a place in His eternal Kingdom. This man, like many, was not open to learning the truth! Holy Scripture says we are *'not saved by our good deeds…'lest any man should boast'* (Ephesians 2:9).

I have found that people who lack a teachable spirit are dogmatic in their opinions and have very legalized religious attitudes as well (sadly including many Christians). They are also likely to be the type that when confronted with a suggestion of change will say, "But, we've always done it this way!" Rigid and uncompromising can also describe them. This even extends to those who will almost never admit they are wrong, even when faced with the evidence! (Another negative trait of my second husband as well!)

I have recently started to respond on the comment section of Fox News articles, and it only takes about three minutes of reading a few postings to realize who the ones without a teachable spirit are! Many regular participants earn my disrespect when it becomes obvious they never adjust their opinions, no matter how often they are presented with verifiable information. Others just re-post the same arguments and never respond without childish name-calling and dismissing anything that contradicts them. (Maybe I need to cut back on my participation as I think it raises my blood pressure.) Still…I can't help reacting to so much misinformation and outright lies, especially when it comes to matters of Christian beliefs!

The photo sent to my brother when our mother lived in NYC.

A Childlike Spirit:

Jesus told His Disciples to allow little children to come to Him when He was teaching. He told them that *'the Kingdom of God was occupied by those who were like a small child'* (Matthew 19:14, paraphrased). All children are born with a natural curiosity and trust, so I believe that is what Jesus wanted His Disciples to understand.

The sad thing is that this chidlike spirit does not seem to last for many of us! Therefore, I think of it as a 'gift' and that God will grant it if we think we are lacking and *ask* for it! However, some, like Claire, seem to have it naturally. A close cousin of mine told me after a family event that she had never met anyone as humble and approachable as Claire. She said Claire was so fun to be with because of her sense of humor, respect for open conversation and sincere caring.

(I would love to receive a compliment like that!) All I have ever met that lacked a teachable spirit are the most narrow-minded, judgmental, quick-to-anger, self-absorbed people! These types are usually somewhat shallow, wanting to discuss only the weather, movies, food, sports, or fashion trends… nothing deeper unless you agree with their viewpoints entirely.

The Reunion:

I am thinking that a close cousin of a teachable spirit might be the willingness to self-examine. In my experience I find that those who lack a teachable spirit are also not prone to do much soul-searching or value introspection in general. I eventually saw evidence of this when the woman who abandoned me and my brothers reappeared in our lives.

I had not seen my mother since she left when I was seven years old. I'm not sure she communicated much with my older brother, but I know he carried a picture of her in his wallet that she sent him after she went to New York. In the picture she had bleached her dark hair to platinum blonde and was wearing a tight-fitting blouse. We did not really talk much about her, but I was told by relatives she had 'babied' him, and I know he was deeply hurt by her leaving. I recall a time shortly after she left when he was sitting on the front steps looking very forlorn, sadly declaring, "I guess this means no more birthday parties." (Our mother was pretty good at creating a fun kid's party, I must admit), but our dad still made sure we each had a party every year anyway.

It wasn't until I was in my fifties when we heard somehow that her second husband had died, and she wanted to come to Seattle to visit us. One of her brothers in Seattle said she would be staying at his home for a few days and wanted us to come there to have a 'reunion'. I was willing and so was my older brother, but our younger brother wanted no part of seeing her at all. (Perhaps it was my younger brother who was the most damaged after all.) I was not as close to him as I was with my older brother, but I know that he had a great distrust of women until he married in his late forties, had his own business and remained childless. I also completely understood his decision to avoid meeting with her.

After a discussion with my older brother, we arranged a day to meet and made reservations to take 'Mom' to lunch after the visit at her brother's home. My sister-in-law came along, and we parked the car in front of the address we were given. Our mother was standing on the front porch to welcome us. Her hair was somewhat long, still blonde, and loosely curled. She was smaller than I expected, wearing a pale peach summer pants outfit, smiling with her arms out to embrace my brother first. I think I heard her say "my baby". I don't remember feeling much emotion, but I found it hard to swallow and my throat felt tight while he shyly accepted her embrace. I still don't remember her reaction to me…it was all very awkward and uncomfortable.

After a brief visit, we left for the restaurant. On the way there, she was chatty in the front seat next to my brother. She also began handing out some costume jewelry to me, explaining how her husband had died from a heart attack while at the racetrack and chuckling about how she was happy without this man she referred to as 'the old pirate'. She told us her other children were adults now, but she had a young granddaughter she was helping to raise, because her daughter was in jail for welfare fraud. I don't remember her asking about my daughter, my brother's kids or why our younger brother was not with us.

After we were seated in the restaurant, she continued to chat, and we exchanged some more small talk while having lunch. After we finished eating, I decided to address the 'elephant in the room' question. I was sitting next to her and simply asked what had made her want to leave our dad and us kids. She turned to me and with a slightly puzzled expression answered, "I really can't say why!"

We visited for a few more minutes before driving her back to her brother's home. She continued to chat about various things going on with her other children and what it was like to live in New York City. When we dropped her off, there were no plans made to get together again before she returned to New York. I have not asked my brother if he continued to contact her, but the only time we heard anything was when she passed away a few years later. One of her other sons called to ask us for some money to pay for her burial. (Apparently Go-Fund-Me was not a thing back then and her other children must have been low-income.) I sent $300.00, and I believe my older brother did the same or more.

On the day I learned she had died, I was at home visiting with two girlfriends. We were having some wine and chatting when the phone rang. After the brief conversation ended, my friends asked what the call was about. I told them my mother had just died. They both looked at each other with shocked expressions, and I remember just smiling and saying it might as well be news that some celebrity just died! I then had to explain that I really had no bond or attachment to this woman who had given me birth. I could tell they were still perplexed at my lack of emotion until I told them about the reunion and the fact that my mother never actually apologized for leaving us and apparently never gave it much thought after more than forty years had passed.

Did my mother lack a 'teachable spirit', and does this include the inability or unwillingness to self-examine? Maybe I should ask a professional psychologist about this. If I were to make an unprofessional diagnosis at this time, I would have to say she could best be described by that popular song from a while back called "Girls Just Want to Have Fun"!

The reason I wonder if this lack of introspection is related to the lack of a teachable spirit is because it seems to go hand-in-hand with many people I have known and others I have read about! These kinds of people are like empty shells, and they never seem to change as they age! I suppose one could say that ignorance is bliss, but in my opinion, it makes them rather shallow and unrelatable.

For what it is worth, the Bible stresses that we need to search our own hearts and meditate on Christ's teachings to truly understand how our thoughts and actions affect others as well as our relationship with Him. I am convinced this results in a more satisfying life! I know, personally, how the lack of these qualities can block forgiveness and the necessary healing for those who have been hurt by others who choose to remain unaware or unwilling to examine themselves.

The Forgiveness Dilemma:

I sometimes wonder if I am the only Christian that questions the teaching that we should always forgive anyone who has done us wrong, including the worst kinds of abuse, even murder. I understand the concept of not harboring hatred and resentment that can cause untold psychological, spiritual, and even physical health damage. And I do agree that there must be a 'letting go' of the hurt or shame to avoid those possible conditions, but I struggle with certain situations of forgiveness and what it should look like.

I know the greatest example that Christians use is while Christ endured the agony of being crucified, he called out to the Father to *'forgive them for they know not what they do'*. Well, it was true that they did not know they were killing the Son of God! Jesus also taught that God is *'not willing that any should perish'*...so maybe this 'forgiveness' would allow them to repent at some point and not go to Hell? (I am speculating here.) However, one cannot avoid the fact that Jesus only forgave the thief dying next to Him who recognized Him as

God's Son, but *not* the other criminal who mocked Him (Luke 23: 32-43 NIV).

Didn't the mocking man also 'not know' what he was doing? I am just not sure if forgiving a non-repentant person is really 'healing' or even if that is what Christ is expecting of us. I am more than willing to forgive *anyone*, even if they severely abused me if I see that they are truly sorry and expressed their regret in some way. I also understand that Christian teaching does not say forgiveness means *forgetting* the wrong or requires us to welcome that person back into our life. The problem I have is my belief that the hurt or resentment would greatly diminish if the person responsible would just admit it and apologize! Here again this would not apply if the person had no idea they hurt you, or if they were dead or otherwise unavailable. (Sigh…am I alone with my thinking on this?) When I apologized to Claire about my neglect during her childhood, I know it brought a healing for both of us. But I also remember the on-going pain of my friend whose father, on his death bed, refused to apologize for his sexual abuse of her. I try to remember to pray for her that she has 'let go' and that she has found peace through Christ if she is still alive.

My second husband desperately wanted me to stay with him but would never admit he was wrong or apologize about his final abusive act that was the 'last straw' for me. I do not wish him, or anyone, an eternity of Hell, but I really prefer to not be around him in eternity. (Wonder if this means I haven't forgiven him?) My first husband actually did admit he had been less of a husband and father than he should have been, and we remained on good terms until he passed away. He had accepted Christ when we were teenagers but strayed far away as many of us do. But Jesus did say that *once we have been given (or 'sent') to Him by the Father that '…no one can snatch them out of my hand'* (John 10:28) so I should not be surprised to see my ex in that Heavenly kingdom.

I have asked God to forgive me for not forgiving, and maybe He will make all this much clearer, perhaps with more meditation on His word? (Otherwise, it will be on my list of questions to ask when my time is up!) I know I have forgiven my mother…because I have no resentment toward her, but no desire to spend time with her in the hereafter either! Again, I do not wish eternal misery on her or anyone; it just would have been healing to know that she recognized the hurt she had caused by her choice to leave as she did. I'm pretty sure, after meeting with her, that her lack of introspection was not intended to be hurtful, just not on her to-do list.

My most fervent prayer is thanking God for a teachable spirit and to ask that He bless my grandchildren with it as well. I know one thing for sure; I have so much to learn. I believe our eternity will be a never-ending journey of learning and I pray for everyone to be blessed with that amazing future!

Chapter 11
SHRAPNEL WOUNDS

Even though I was blessed to have dodged the '60s bullet, I did not escape some of the shrapnel! This shrapnel included the mantra of that time: AKA If it feels good, do it!' and it also brought other liberal, unbiblical teachings that infected many traditional churches. Even my blessed grandparents' teachings were not enough to keep me completely protected from these wounds. Unfortunately, the 'collateral' damage continues.

Scripture says that *God chastens those He loves* (Hebrews 12:6-9). As I look back on certain events in my life, I realize now how much He must *really* love me! Actually, there is a very good chance my life would have ended when Claire was only 2 years old if not for the fact that God apparently loved me enough to have other plans for me!

When I was about 27 years old and Claire was a toddler, I am now embarrassed to admit I was fond of going out to a neighborhood country and western tavern with a friend on Friday nights. My friend's parents would babysit, and I would help her with her hair and makeup before we went out. I justified this because my husband always worked nights and I had begun to feel, and act, like I deserved a good time.

The best thing about this place was the band that sometimes let me sing! They called themselves *'Jerry Jack Adams and the Country Rebels'*. They were pretty good, and once in a while I would also get asked to dance! My friend was always hoping to get 'hooked up' for the night, but I was happy to just be out with some adult company.

One night my friend left with a guy she'd met so I left by myself to go to my car and pick up Claire. I was totally sober (thank God) walking to my car that was parked across the street at a closed gas station. There were several other cars with patrons about to leave. (My car was a brand new two-door, bright yellow, V-8 Mustang Fastback we called the 'Yellow Banana'.) As soon as I started to open the door, my wrist and keys were grabbed from behind by a tall, skinny white dude wearing horn-rimmed glasses, trembling and yelling at me to "Get in the car!" My first reaction was shock, and I thought that he was scared and needed help! I asked him what was wrong, and he just kept pushing me and demanding through clenched teeth to "Shut up and get in the car!" He was over six feet and had pushed himself into the driver's seat with me almost straddling the gear area while he tried to start the car. I pleaded with him that I had a child to pick up, but he clamped his hand over my mouth while yelling, "Shut up or I'll kill you right here!"

So much for wondering if this was really a bad guy! It was all happening so fast, and I knew I had to get focused. I had heard that if anyone manages to drive away with you in a car…all bets are off. I made up my mind that I was not going to die this way and looked for a way to escape. He had let go of my mouth and was trying to start the car. One thing that saved me was the way the car had to be started. The key had to be turned and held firmly to the right while pumping the gas enough to start the engine (1970 model) and he was struggling with it. The next thing in my favor was the width and weight of the doors. I knew that if I could just get that passenger door open, it would swing wide out and it could not be closed unless you could reach far enough to grab the handle and bring it back!

At this point, I could not have cared less about the car, my purse or all the keys (to everything) …*nothing* but getting away! I saw this moment as my only possible chance, and with every ounce of strength I could muster, I started pumping my '70s style, two-inch block-heeled shoes into the side of his leg. I somehow managed to scramble over the passenger seat and force the door open! I lunged over the side, landing with my elbows on the parking lot cement! I was gasping for breath but got on my feet and banged on the nearest car for help, to no avail. Not looking back (as I felt he was right behind me) I ran across the street and barged through the double doors of the tavern, screaming for someone to help me!

The bartender (or manager) was cleaning up to close for the night. He calmly handed me a towel, telling me my mouth was bleeding. I was hysterical, trying to explain what was happening and asked one of the waitresses for a dime to call the police, but no one would give me one! (Yes, that was the cost of a pay phone then, and I found out later that they did not want any 'trouble' due to other incidents, so no dime!)

I kept pleading to the few people still around that there was a guy out there trying to kidnap and kill me! Soon two guys and a young woman offered to escort me out to my car. I told them NO, *I needed the police!* They kept insisting as I was sobbing and resisting their efforts to pull me out of the tavern. They finally succeeded, and when we got to my car, the guy was gone along with the keys. The doors were open, and my purse was still there, but I had no way to get home or pick up Claire! I told them my husband was at work and had a set of keys, so they insisted that they take me to get them so I could get my car to drive home. These three 'Good Samaritans' turned out to be from another Country band and I decided to trust them. (One of the guys took the carburetor out in case the creep came back to get the car.)

To make this long story a little shorter, we got back, and the guys replaced the carburetor so I was able to drive home. I then called my friend's parents to see if they could keep Claire until the next day and they said yes…then I waited up until my husband came home to tell him what had happened. (He had not reacted much to my experience or asked to leave work when I showed up that night, but just gave me the keys!) As I said previously, we did not have much of a marriage.

My husband was six feet three inches and very buff. I was five feet four inches and about 130 pounds, but when I described what happened and demonstrated how this jerk had pushed me, he lost his balance and fell to the floor from the force I used! (I think my adrenalin was still up.)

By now it was around 8:30 a.m., and I called the police to report what happened. An officer arrived after about a half hour. I described my attacker as best as I could; guessing his age around early twenties, over six feet tall and thin with a black afro, though he was white, clean-shaven and wearing nerdy, black-rimmed glasses.

After I finished with the rest of the details, the officer said the description sounded like a guy they were looking for known as the Bellevue Rapist. (At this time the police were also dealing with the Green River Killer and Ted Bundy.) As far as I know they never found this guy, but I told them to watch for a guy who looked like my attacker, limping pretty badly or possibly in a hospital after I showed them the inside of the car. The thick rubber floor mat on the driver's side was ripped through by the force of my wooden heels while kicking him. By this time my husband was no longer wondering if I was for real about what happened. He even decided to call his football buddy and wife to go with us later that night to talk to the tavern manager about the 'dime' refusal.

When we walked in, the four of us must have made an impression because it was obvious we weren't there for the entertainment. When my husband asked about their refusal to help me, the bartender claimed they were too worried about the police being called, and all the waitresses just looked nervous and walked away.

Well, needless to say, my singing-career fantasies with the band were over. I never set foot in that place again, much to the disappointment of my tavern-buddy girlfriend. And one would think my 'single life' pursuits were also over, but God was not done with His 'love' for me and the lessons I still needed to learn.

More Chastening:

Every time I looked in the mirror after that, I noticed a small bubble that formed over the cut on my lower lip from the force of this jerk's hold over my mouth that night. It was many years later that a dentist offered to refer me for its removal. I decided to have it done, but there is a slight trace of a bump still there. One thing I found out about myself was how righteous anger and adrenalin can produce enough physical strength to fight off an attack! I also learned to never be casual when alone at night...*anywhere!*

However, my next lesson would not be at night, but in broad daylight. I was still a CINO (Christian In Name Only) acting like I was not married by going out with my unmarried girlfriends after work for an early Happy Hour.

We got off at 3:30 and usually walked a block or so to a local hangout. I would always leave to go home and be with Claire by 5:30 though. One time my friends left me with a much older, gray-bearded man who was listening to me sympathetically as I was getting emotional about my mother's abandonment. One of my friends had been pressuring me to get some counseling for several weeks (I think because *she* was in counseling) so, after a couple of drinks, I was pouring out my soul to this dude. He claimed to be a professor of psychology at the nearby college. When I said I needed to leave, he offered to take me to my car which was parked by the hotel I worked in. But he insisted I experience the new sound system he just had bought for his truck. I was tired and anxious to leave so I said okay.

After we listened to some music, he proceeded to drive the opposite way from where I had parked, so I asked him to let me out. He kept driving, and I kept demanding him to stop and let me out! He then yelled some profanities and pushed me out of the truck onto the main road, where I landed face down with my purse scattered about a yard or so in front of me!

For some reason there was almost no traffic, and I looked up to see two very large black men hovering over me! They bent down to help me up asking, "What happened, mama?" I told them about the guy, and that I just needed to get to my car and go home. They offered to take me to my car, and for some reason I felt I could trust them! When I got in my car, they said they wanted to follow me, as they knew I had been drinking and were worried. I thanked them but told them I was fine. They persisted in wanting to follow me for my safety… so I agreed, and again felt I could trust them.

It took about ten minutes or so to drive home. I parked in front of my house, and they said they would leave as soon as I was safely inside. They did as they said. I wish now I had gotten their names in order to properly thank them for their kindness. I could only surmise these two were most likely University of Washington athletes who just happened to be walking in the area I was dumped off in. Or were they?

Entertaining Angels:

Hebrews 13: 2 (KJV) says, *"Be not forgetful to entertain strangers: for thereby some have entertained angels unawares."*

I have since wondered about this possibility, not only for what happened this time, but perhaps on other occasions when I was where I shouldn't be. There are many news stories of very narrow escapes and unlikely survivals…especially of children, and scripture does speak of *'guardian angels'* for them as well. (Why so many children are killed or suffer will be one of my questions for God…but then, angels also have free will and God's purposes are often a mystery for now.) Angels can appear as human, as when Mary was told of her forthcoming conception of Jesus. When Jesus had risen and left the tomb he had been placed in, an angel was seated in the tomb telling the women who came to tend the body that He had risen. (An interesting thing is that every angel in scripture is *only* described as male.) Angels have supernatural powers that we humans lack, but they also have free will and a third of them rebelled and followed Satan…but more on that later as scripture warns to *"Test every spirit to see if it is of God"* (1 John 4: 1-3).

I did not report this last incident to the police, but I should have. I think I was just too embarrassed at my bad judgment to even tell anyone about it. I found out later that this jerk did work at the U of W but was not a professor. He was just an old bar *'regular'* that hung out to pick up stupid women like me.

The shrapnel from the '60s bullet affected many like me who should have been better equipped spiritually to heal faster or escape being grazed in the first place! The truth is I am as human and flawed as anyone else who is still around. I have also been affected by the moral decay that has not abated since. But I have learned that God's love is as faithful as He promises in His Holy word! I am certainly not the same unwise soul I was before He schooled me! And because I was blessed by my grandparents' quiet but obvious Christian example of right and wrong. I'm sure this is why I did not suffer a fatal hit!

At this point in my life, I am hoping to at least make sure my grandchildren know what I have experienced, and maybe someone reading this book will benefit from the lessons God chastened me with! I have come to believe we are possibly living in what scripture calls *'the end times'*…meaning the period of time before Christ returns for His own before the world has accepted the dictator (AKA the *Antichrist*) who rules for seven horrific years over mankind. There is much written about this, so I will leave most of this subject to the many experts in Bible literature and the prophecy available to anyone interested.

I am thinking now more about the 'prophecy' my German immigrant, former Mennonite grandfather spoke of before the '60s bullet hit America. Unfortunately, it was also a shot felt around the world! America is not alone in experiencing the moral decay that the '60s rebellion brought to the fore, but perhaps God is using it to separate the wheat from the chaff?

Maybe my grandfather's premonition was a God-given glimpse of what we are witnessing now as a prelude to His righteous reckoning with His creation during the seven years of Antichrist rule, also known as the *'Great Tribulation'*?

Chapter 12
LIBERTY OR LICENSE

According to the New Oxford American Dictionary, *Liberty* is defined as: "The state of being free within society from oppressive restrictions imposed by authority on ones' way of life, behavior or political views" (a partial definition, but generally accepted as applicable).

License, according to the same dictionary, is defined as: "Formal or official permission to do something; or *freedom to behave as one wishes; or a reason to excuse or do something wrong or excessive.*" (It also includes the Old French from the Latin *'Licentiousness'* that is inferred when used to describe moral laxity).

The dictionary is much more extensive in defining these terms, but I do not need to include all of it in this instance. *License*, in the way my grandfather used it, is referring to immoral or anti-established norms of social behavior being acceptable. *Liberty*, as he saw it, was simply the kind of freedom our founding fathers meant it to be, and also how scripture uses it. The Bible describes it as the *freedom to overcome sin by our trust in His son, Jesus, as Savior.* It further assures us that although we still have our sinful nature, we are no longer a *slave* to it. This *freedom* is backed up by the added blessing Jesus gave us when He sent His *Holy Spirit* to reside in the hearts of believers, and it is that Spirit that helps us resist the temptations to do wrong.

Another aspect of what my grandfather feared is the difference between *legal* and *moral* behavior. After the '60s sexual revolution, some things that were previously illegal were no longer so! Male homosexual intimate relations (sodomy) became legal; divorce for any reason…previously only allowed for adultery, became legal; gambling became legal in most states and drinking to excess is only illegal if you are driving while intoxicated or causing a public disturbance. A baby conceived outside of marriage was 'illegitimate', and the child was labeled a *BASTARD* on its birth certificate. That was rightfully stopped, thanks to the efforts of true Christians. (The baby was not guilty of any sin and that labeling was totally immoral.)

There are many things that are legal and tolerated, but still considered by many to be immoral or wrong…such as fornication (sexual intercourse without marriage), same-sex marriage, pornography, 'recreational' marijuana use, alcohol abuse and now the growing use of heroin and other hard drugs that might as well be legal. Even more disturbing is the newest drug with unprecedented deadly results coming across our southern border from China called fentanyl.

In my opinion, right now, some of the worst legal drugs of all are the hormone blockers used to alter one's gender, especially for *CHILDREN*! (More on this later.)

Harmful, but not illegal, includes the current homeless issue, with people turning city streets into sewers of sex-trafficking, addiction, assaults, and robberies as well as property and environmental damage! Another example is the suffering that results from being in debt, which has not been illegal for centuries (debtor's prisons were once accepted as necessary!) …but is being in debt a good thing? Cigarettes are legal…but a good thing to spend money on and harm your health with? Over-charging people for goods and services is not *illegal,* in general, but it hurts the poor and working class, and God's Word says it is not okay with HIM! (Proverbs 11:1).

Then we have the 'Mother of All' legal-but-immoral example…abortion. It became legal in the United States by the Supreme Court decision regarding the case of Roe v. Wade in 1973. This became the biggest *license* to be sexually irresponsible ever approved by human law! This decision was celebrated by women and men who engage in fornication but want to get rid of the possible results of their sexual gratification. I realize I am generalizing, but it actually is the main reason for defending this practice. It is sad when a woman is pregnant from rape or incest…but this is rare, and the baby had nothing to do with the crime! There are many of these babies who became wonderful additions to this world and are very glad they were not aborted in those cases! Even imperfect babies have been a blessing to many parents. *'My body…my choice'* is a LIE because the baby is NOT the woman's body and has no choice!

The evil of legalizing abortion can be seen in the diminishing value of life we are witnessing now. The 'My body…my choice' arrogance reduces the growing fetus to an inconvenience, and this reality is not missed by the generations since Roe v. Wade. I once worked with a man who was old enough to know better, but he defended abortion by claiming that life does not begin at conception and is not even human until born. I showed him an online photo of a five-week-old embryo, and all he said was "See? It is just a BEAN!" (He was a college grad in computer tech and a military veteran...and remained adamant about his opinion.)

I believe the legalization of abortion is the main reason we have a growing callousness to taking a life by younger and younger teens and the adults they are learning from. When this decision was added to the teaching that we are not created beings, but simply evolved from a swamp-dwelling amoeba of some kind, evil took an even stronger foothold.

Another False Religion:

The '60s attempt to confuse *liberty* with *license* is to acknowledge that the real 'rebellion' was not just against the establishment, but against God, the Creator of humanity and nature.

This belief is called *humanism* and has become another false religion and one of the most damaging wounds to cripple the victims of the '60s bullet. This is the rejection of God and the belief that we humans can make everything better by relying on our own devises and intelligence. A perfect example of this was when society decided that *feminism* was the best way for women to feel empowered. Men were soon dismissed as irrelevant in the raising of children because women could 'do it all' they said! Well, we can all see how well that has played out, can't we? Unfortunately, we are still doing this today by continuing to exalt women who are single moms, many by choice, like it is an honor. Of course, there are many wonderful single mothers who have managed to raise great kids...but the message that this is just as good as a mom and dad family goes against God's intended plan for our happiness.

Not only has NOW (National Organization of Women) and the so-called Feminist Movement damaged marriages, but it is also responsible for crushing the spirit of boys who are becoming wounded adult males today! They ranted for years about how 'patriarchal' (and therefore damaging) it was to let boys play Cowboys and Indians, Cops and Robbers or GI Joe and Army games. Then they embraced the idea that boys needed to be 'calmed down' with ADHD drugs so they could behave more like the girls in school! Now here in 2022 the 'Wokesters' are insisting that all toy stores mix their toys as unisex on their shelves! All this to deny that males were created by God to be stronger, more assertive and able to protect and serve their country as well as provide for and protect a wife and children!

There was a study some years ago that revealed the truth about male and female natural differences. The researchers put several toddlers of both genders in a large room full of toys for them to play with. They then ran a tape to record what happened. The boys chose all the 'boy' toys and the girls played with the 'girl' toys. (No surprise.) Then they did a different study with the girls in a room with only toys designed for boys and the boys in a room with only 'girl' toys. When they finished the filming, it showed something not quite expected. The little girls were seen using their coats or sweaters for blankets to wrap the trucks in for a nap and rocking the GI-Joes in their arms! The boys were seen making guns out of the Barbie's legs and bodies, pretending to shoot each other; and running around throwing doll furniture back and forth. The boys would also stack the girl toys as high as they could and then smash them down with whatever they found to destroy them with! (This experiment should be a mandatory teaching subject for every student studying for a degree in psychology…or any humanity-related degree, IMHO.)

There is so much wrong sauce on all of this denial of the male purpose and their masculine qualities! It is NATURAL and GOOD for boys to build (and defend) forts, to climb trees, dig in the dirt, wrestle and race against each other! They are not designed to sit quietly at a desk when they are in school all day! They need longer recesses and more physical activities than girls do! We need to stop this mistreatment, adjust the curriculum and be grateful for the way God made males, PERIOD! (It's my soap-box and I'll rant if I want to!)

We also need to face the fact that men are physically stronger and far more able to lift and carry an adult to safety! Be grateful that a male swimmer can get to a victim faster and have more strength to help a flailing, drowning child or adult! Of course, many women are valuable in almost all areas of first re-sponders and military service, etc. …but if I need help against an attacker, an accident or fire, I am going to feel much better if a man is coming to the rescue! And regarding those child studies you might think, well…nature or nurture, but I think it was clear that boys and girls are not just physically different, but emotionally and mentally as well. That is how God intended it… and it is a GOOD thing!

Dads Wanted:

Nothing is more revealing than the fact that almost every male behind bars (and most females) either had no father in their lives, or one who was a useless or immoral jerk, and often a criminal as well.

Several years ago, I watched a TV show about a group of male veterans who wanted to help kids who were on the wrong path in life, similar to the *Scared Straight* program where juveniles are confronted by actual prisoners and presented with the realities of jail time. In this show it featured a tall, muscular man in uniform getting loud and angry at a boy who looked about 11 or 12 years old. The man was bent forward while yelling in the kid's face, "Do you want someone like me on your case everyday boy!" The child remained stoic… just staring straight ahead while the man kept on screaming things like, "You want ME forcing you to do what I want?! You want ME breathing down your neck like this all the time…well, DO YOU?" At that point the boy looked up with tears streaming down his face and loudly blurted out, *"YES!"*

As big and tough as this man was, he had to abruptly turn away so the boy would not see the tears welling up in his own eyes.

This is reality. This is the damage we have allowed to remain and grow since the '60s bullet made a direct hit on the male psyche by the so-called *Women's Liberation* movement. It was a mantra of this movement that *"A woman needs a man like a fish needs a bicycle."* Gloria Steinem made this remark and had a massive following of young women who bought into the whole notion that they could *'do and have it all'* without a male in their life or their children's lives.

Then the '60s *War on Poverty* policies made things worse when our government decided they could help poor families by supporting women if they had children; but only if they were not married and had no 'father figure' in the home. Now we see the horrendous results with the gangs that fatherless boys (and many young girls) seek out for the missing dads, discipline, and family security in their lives.

I also believe this anti-male cancer is at the root of the whole 'gender-fluid' lie being foisted on society now. As far as I am concerned this is *Satanic* in origin…about as evil as the sexual abuse of children and the emotional or physical abuse of any human.

This movement to blur the differences between males and females has morphed into the insanity of the belief that humans can change their biology and become the opposite sex! (Another fall-out from the religion of *humanism* and the rejection of a Creator God).

Controlling Nature:

Another '60s legacy of the religion of *humanism* is that we can also control the Earth's nature! The movement to fight pollution started out as a very righteous effort. As believers, both Jews and Gentiles are told in scripture that we are to be *'stewards'* of the earth. God said we were to have *'dominion'* over all living creatures and the land, with the understanding that it was a gift from Him that required our constant respect and care. (This is all spelled out in the first book of the Bible, Genesis.)

Thanks to our human nature to mess things up, this movement soon morphed into a cult of what some are now calling *Nature Nazis*. These folks mandate endless rules against the common- sense of things like proper forest management! Our timber industry was vastly damaged over an owl they believed was going extinct! Many other harmful restrictions, regarding too many critters to list here, have caused so much personal, ecological, and financial harm that it is a wonder our entire eco system has not completely imploded! Here in 2022, they are still claiming that Co2 is the cause of climate change (AKA global warming)! Co2! Carbon dioxide…the very thing we exhale that without it, all plant life would die! There is counter-information available by so many climate experts and scientific studies that disprove all this, but I will leave that to the reader's desire to learn more. What's disturbing is the reality that there are far too many who sincerely believe that we humans have the power to radically alter the nature of God's creation!

Worshiping Nature:

Nature itself has also become a 'god' for too many today…but it is not a new phenomenon. Many ancient religions required the worship of *creation*: humans, animals, or the Earth itself. Wickens, Pagans and New-Agers are examples of these religious cults today. I recently worked with a lady who was a proud Pagan, and she is a nature-lover who is also fine with abortion! These cult followers reject the existence of a Divine Creator, including any eternal life consequences, and also believe that human life is no more important than a tree or a frog. (I wonder if these current cultists are aware that the ancient Pagans worshiped their various gods by throwing babies onto a flaming alter to be burned alive as a sacrifice, or if they would care.)

I recently saw photos of several *'worshipers'* confessing their sins and pledging their faith to a room full of plants. They believe God is *'in all things'*, which is not at all biblical…but believed by many. The Creator is *not* His creation… God is not 'in' the mosquito that bites us, or in the burger we eat, or in the ferns that grow! The biblical declaration that God only created *humans* in *His image*, and that only *He* is to be *worshiped* is rejected by these folks. As silly as all this sounds it is accepted by many and will eventually morph into the false World Religion that will emerge before the Antichrist takes control. It will be a religion that is a melting pot of teaching that *'all beliefs lead to Heaven'* and anyone who disagrees will be selected for persecution. The Antichrist will be a ruthless world dictator, but he will have a 'priestly partner' who will bring in this new world religion. The Antichrist will use this religion in order to demand worship of himself as 'God' before the end of his seven-year reign. (2nd Thessalonians 2:4 and Revelations 13:12)

There is so much on this subject that anyone interested can learn, and I am not qualified as a Bible or religious scholar to expound on it any further here. I am just grateful for the promises of Christ that His plans will prevail and all who choose to know Him will be spared the evil He warns will come exactly as prophesied. This is what true *'liberty'* is about, the freedom of knowing the TRUTH, not the *'license'* of a Godless society bent on self-gratification and the lies we often choose to believe.

Chapter 13
BACK TO THE FUTURE

Going back now to the future my grandfather was concerned about in 1963, it is obvious to me that he must have had a gift of prophecy. Scripture says many will have this gift in the end times. I know people have been declaring *'The end is near'* for centuries, but it needs to be noted that scripture also tells us that *'Our ways are not His ways, and our thoughts are not His thoughts'* as well as *'A day is like a thousand years and a thousand years is like a day to the Lord'*…so there's that to consider (2nd Peter 3: 8). So, as far as Almighty God is concerned it's only been a few days, and scripture also says He is in no hurry to bring the hammer down and wants all to turn to Him and be part of His Kingdom!

The liberty my grandfather was speaking of is actually the liberty we enjoy by allowing God's Holy Spirit, through Christ, to help us resist our natural free will to embrace evil. (Scripture describes it as *no longer being a slave to our sin nature*, as stated in Romans 6: 1-7). Jesus said when we accept His gift of redemption He sends us a 'comforter' to dwell in us; this is the third part of the Trinity…the Holy Spirit of God. But just as with God-the-Father, we have the free will to reject the Holy Spirit's guidance. Scripture tells us that this 'grieves' Him. We are told *'Do not grieve the Holy Spirit'* (Ephesians 4: 30) … something I am sure I have done many times myself. This, again, is why I am *so* grateful for forgiveness!

My Christian understanding is still a work-in-progress, but the evidence of God's truth is so overwhelming that I have a hard time understanding the continued rebellion against it! I like to read the comment sections of news articles and respond to any that claim there is no evidence of what some call the "Sky Fairy", as well as the ones who don't even believe Jesus existed!

I rarely get a response when I simply ask them if they understand why the world's calendar started over with year #1 being His *birth year* if He didn't even exist! I wish this fact was taught to every school child…the fact that the year 2022 means it has been two thousand and twenty-two years since Jesus was born! I can absolutely guarantee that the calendar will not start over with my birth year, no matter how famous I become! Apparently this was decided about 500 years after He was crucified, but a pretty significant historical fact! Then there's that historically scientific dating thing… like the years before year one are called BC…*before Christ*! In fact, scholars have proved that there is actually more evidence of the existence of Jesus than any other human in recorded history!

I also challenge unbelievers to consider the fact that the Bible does not contain any lies, and every prophecy up until now has been fulfilled except for the war described in Ezekiel 38 and the events that will precede the Antichrist and the seven-year Tribulation. These events include the 'catching up' or rapture of Christ's believers (His 'bride', the Church)! And there is absolutely no doubt in my mind that these prophecies will also be fulfilled!

Scripture also warns there will be many who will reject the Bible and the true God it speaks of. We are told by Jesus to just *'shake the dust off our feet'* and not stress over their rejection but pray they open their hearts and minds at some point. He also said: *'Do not caste pearls before swine' and 'Do not give what is holy to dogs'* (Matthew 7: 6). He was a realist about those who would reject Him and did not want His followers to waste their efforts!

The *future* my grandfather 'feared' is what the '60s bullet has produced. I have tried to describe how it has actually played out in my observations, but it should also be evident to any reader that has been paying attention. One thing I want to make clear is that although I dodged its trajectory, I did not escape the shrapnel…none of us has. I was blessed by my date of birth, so I avoided the direct hit, unlike many who were born just a few years after me. I did not completely buy into every cultural trend because I also had the example of my immigrant Christian grandparents. Those without the influence of a morally strong upbringing are extremely blessed if their wounds are only superficial!

As I look back now, my only question concerning my grandparents was why they never expected their children to attend a Christian church service (that I can recall). They had a daughter who eventually became a Christian scientist/New-Ager and my dad was a life-long agnostic. One of his brothers also became a New-Ager, one was Episcopalian and another became a Catholic later in life. Someday, when I see them again, I will ask about this! I also regret not insisting that Claire attend Sunday school when she was a child, because it can only help to have a basic understanding of Bible teachings and it might have influenced her as a teen and young adult. (By God's grace, she did eventually invite Christ into her heart.)

In thinking more about my agnostic dad, I am still perplexed that he most likely remained that way until he died, because he was already very 'Christian' in so many ways! One of the thoughtful things I remember him doing was when he painted the ceiling of the bedroom I shared with my younger brother after our mother left. He painted it a very dark blue and put decals of stars and a moon on it that glowed in the dark! (My dad thought we would like to look up at it and feel like we were sleeping outside.) So many things he did for us, without a wife to help, I now realize were a sacrifice of his love for us that few single parents manage to do! This memory came to me before writing this chapter and it makes me wonder, and pray, that God has included him in His kingdom after all. My father was a thoughtful, caring man, and none of us know what anyone has in their heart when they die…only God knows.

There are times when I truly wish the Catholic belief in Purgatory was supported by scripture! A place where non-believers reside after death until they realize the truth they rejected during their Earthly life! This concept is never mentioned by Jesus or any of the disciples and is not found in the Torah or Old Testament at all. Scripture does assure us that God's justice is perfect and that now we only *see through a glass darkly* but we will have complete understanding when we pass over to eternity (1st Corinthians 13:12).

The only important question now regarding Jesus is whether or not we believe He is who He claimed to be! He was tortured and killed because He would not deny His Oneness with God. All of His disciples were crucified, stoned to death, or imprisoned for life because they would not deny the deity and claims of this 'man'. Every human who knows about Jesus will need to decide if He is the true, living God or was the most influential faker in all of history. His Holy word says this must be decided before our last breath, and this is pretty critical since our eternal destination depends on it! Having free will does not mean we are free from consequences, and any *opinions* that God, Heaven and Hell are not real are of no relevance to Him whatsoever.

I do not have the intellect or Bible education like a C.S. Lewis, or a Billy Graham, but I believe the Holy Scriptures are true and without mistakes…an incredible God-breathed collection of history, wisdom and prophecy, and I am not about to gamble against it! I have friends and relatives that are still on the fence spiritually, or are not even interested in considering this eternal decision. This breaks my heart because I want them to be there with their talents and personalities in an endless journey of learning, exploring, and doing all they have ever longed to do! We might even be able to time-travel, because scripture says we will have bodies like Christ Himself!

I love thinking about the things I enjoy most about my Earth time, like being in a play, writing a screenplay or even doing some stand-up comedy. I also would love to design clothing (DNA from Mom?) or being able to have a pet lamb or any animal of my choice! Of course this will also include the joy of reuniting with relatives or friends that got there before me and meeting people like Abraham Lincoln, Moses, and so many fascinating historical people! The possibilities will be endless, and scripture says we will all be in positions of service and/or authority as assigned by Christ Himself. Our bodies will be at their peak, and without weariness in that incredible Kingdom. There is so much in the Bible about this as well as many other scholarly writings that will inspire any reader to explore what I am not prepared to write about here!

Another fun thing my granddaughter and I have discussed is some of the questions we might want to ask God about. Her first one will be how come so many men (and all giraffes) have prettier, thicker eye lashes than us girls? I agree, and that includes deer's eyes and most cows as well! (I am hoping better eyelashes will be part of my new body.) I will also ask Him what the purpose of slugs was, other than making the slug bait people rich! Another thing I want to know is *why* is everything that we love to eat not healthy for us? I personally would have four or five malted milkshakes every day if they weren't so fattening! *And,* how come some people could eat all they want and stay trim while others living on three twigs and a bowl of dirt are obese? (I do believe God has a great sense of humor, so that conversation should be fun!)

Well, according to scripture, after the seven-year *Great Tribulation*, the thousand-year *'Millennium'* here on Earth will be a bug and slug-free, disease-free, evil-free environment when Christ returns. We who were raptured before the Tribulation will be in our new, immortal bodies, assisting Jesus in His Divine Rule over the remnant of people who turned to Christ and survived that unspeakable, horrific time of judgment! At the end of that thousand years there will be a final, brief battle when Satan himself and all his forces will be put in their *eternal* place of torment. It is then that our eternity begins in the new Heaven and the new Earth! As I mentioned before, I can only offer a brief overview of this *good news* (Gospel) and share my joy of knowing that those who admit their sinful nature and accept Jesus for all He claimed to be will experience this promise!

Another thing that supports my belief in the truth of God's word is when I realized a possible meaning of the claim that humans were created in the 'image' of God! As I was questioning this, it occurred to me that we are also a 'trinity'! Are we not mind, body and spirit, just as God is? Of course not equal to, but *'in His image'*? (I might be thinking above my pay- grade here, but it makes sense to me!)

Well, an easy and uplifting read on all this is a recent book by Greg Laurie titled *REVELATION, A Book of Promises*.

If you can't deal with tackling the whole Bible on your own, this is a worthwhile way to spend some time to understand the basic truth and joy of God's word.

CHAPTER 14
MY MOST SHAMEFUL SINS

This page left intentionally blank

With all due respect, can I say NOYB? Sorry, but God already knows every single awful act, thought or word I am guilty-as-charged with, so I will exercise *my* free will to leave it with Him! I still am awestruck by His promise that whatever we confess and repent-of will not only be forgiven but *forgotten* by Him! I feel so unworthy, and so overwhelmed with this that I constantly pray for help to let go of these regrets. I shared these thoughts with someone in my church, and she assured me I am not alone in this struggle to accept this gift and forgive myself! I know that God understands these human feelings, but I also know it 'grieves' His Holy Spirit when we do not 'let go' of what He has let go of! (I intend to ask about this also, as I am not so sure we *are* expected to not remember or feel regretful despite being forgiven.)

In fact, I always marvel at people who claim to have 'no regrets'! There are T-shirts, bumper stickers and tattoos that say this! I have to assume that those who display that are probably not Christians or at least haven't done much soul-searching! I just cannot imagine anyone living past the age of 7 not making a few life choices that were regrettable…at least by God's standards! I don't think I've actually met someone who is that devoid of self-awareness, although my mother might fit that description. Even then, only God knew her heart when she took her last earthly breath.

I do know that scripture states the self-righteous and unrepentant will not be part of the amazing eternal life He has planned for those who have accepted His gift of forgiveness.

Chapter 15
A TIME OF CHOOSING

I am currently, in 2022, experiencing more Bible prophecy events than I ever thought I would witness! And the fact that all previous prophecies have been fulfilled up to the time before Christ will reappear is another reason to be sure all God's promises will be kept!

In the book of Matthew, chapter 24, verses 3-29, we can read what Jesus said the signs of His coming would be. (Paraphrasing this will sound more like the headlines we are being bombarded with now.) He said there would be *'wars and rumors of wars, famines, earthquakes, pestilence (disease), intense weather and natural disasters.'* He said there will be *'many false Christs and to not be deceived.'* He added that these things will be the *'beginning of birth pangs, but to not fear because they must take place.'*

'Lawlessness will increase and the love of many will grow cold' (a truth we are witnessing daily now!) Other scriptures say it will be a time of a great *'falling away'* from the true faith (Matthew 24: 10) and *'good will be called evil and evil good'* in the end times. All we need to observe this are the constant assaults on the simple truth of biology and science; as in the insistence that gender is only a societal construct and 'fluid'. It's like every day is *Backwards Day!* It's as if Orwell's book, 1984, is being played out before our eyes. Never in my lifetime has this assault on truth been as prevalent as we've seen in the past few years! The main reason I believe we may be living in the 'end times' is because even though these things have been happening throughout history, they have not been occurring as frequently or as intensely as they are now. Jesus said *this time would be obvious, like a woman in labor when the pains come closer together, with more intensity just before the birth.*

These are some of the warnings Jesus told His followers so they would not be caught off guard and be ready for his return, not to the Earth yet, but to *rapture* them (catch them up) before the judgment gets serious! If you read the book of Revelation, you will see what John 'saw' when he was spiritually transported to witness the events that would take place during this time of judgment on the Earth. (I'm not sure if the scariest movie ever made could prepare humanity to accept what John was shown.)

The hardest part of all this is learning that millions will reject God's plan of escape and choose to believe the lies of Satan, the Antichrist and his false prophet. Those left behind will face unbelievable horror. (Some will actually repent, but most of them will not survive…some will, but more on that later.)

A Flashback:

Another thing Jesus mentions prior to the Antichrist's appearance are the *'signs and lying wonders'* (2 Thessalonians 2:9 KJV) that will also be happening then. I believe the current up-tick in attention to UFO sightings is possibly involved in this prophecy. I am flashing back to when my father was obsessed with UFOs. He belonged to a group of men, equally obsessed, who called themselves the APRG (Aerial Phenomena Research Group). This was headed by a local firefighter when I was a teen. My dad brought me to the meetings, and they appointed me the minutes taker! They were a nice bunch; a little odd, but always gracious and friendly. We gathered in the firefighter's basement where there was wall after wall of huge maps covered with various colored push-pins that indicated where and when the UFO sightings were reported.

Sometimes the latest 'personal contact' news story was discussed, and it was always a weird and unpleasant encounter that was described. I did not get too involved in the whole thing, and now I am thinking these sightings and encounters are likely a part of the demonic deception predicted. Many people who claim to have close experiences with aliens say the 'messages' they receive from them is always the same…that they are 'superior beings' and our traditional beliefs in religion, especially Christianity are false. (These same messages are common with cultic spiritual 'contacts' by those who follow so-called mystics.)

I am also concerned that the growing interest in UFOs is laying the groundwork for the Antichrist to claim the rapture of Christians was not by Christ, as stated in the Bible, but by these 'superior beings' who came to save our planet from these people who were in the way of the Utopia he is trying to create. Trust me; this is being promoted by many of the One-World folks as I write! Jesus warned us to *'not be deceived'* during the time prior to the Great Tribulation, and I am convinced we are at the beginning of that time. These 'lying signs and wonders' will likely include many other happenings designed by our increasing technology in order to convince the world of the legitimacy of the Antichrist ruler.

Some Good News:

This brings me to the subject of mortality, AKA *death*. We all have heard over and over again the statement "No one gets out of here alive". Well, if you are a true believer in Jesus, you know that is not true! Millions *will* be alive when Christ returns for those who put their trust in Him; and they will be taken off the Earth before (or perhaps during) the seven-year 'Great Tribulation'. This prophecy can actually happen at any moment, since everything has already occurred as predicted before the rapture can take place. (However, I personally believe we might witness the war against Israel described in Ezekiel 38 before that happens, or possibly by the mid-point of the Tribulation as some are debating now.) Today's headlines are reporting the possibility that Israel could be attacked by all the nations described in that Bible prophecy! This war will be for the energy and resources these countries want as well as the goal of Iran (Persia) to eliminate Israel. I would love to witness the awesome power of God when He intervenes to protect the 'apple of His eye'! With our technology today, the whole world will be able to witness this! (Ezekiel's description is a mind-boggling read for anyone interested!)

There are many Christian churches today that are not telling the truth about how important Israel is! Jesus told the Samaritan woman, "*Salvation is of the Jews*" (John 4: 19-22). Even so, some claiming to be true followers of Christ are even teaching that Israel has been replaced by the Christian church! God's Holy Word says, '*He will bless those who bless Israel and curse those who curse Israel!*' (Genesis 12:3). I believe to ignore this will not go well with any professing Christian when they stand before Him. Again, we are wise to follow the advice of Christ to not be deceived and to trust in His word.

We are also blessed because the Bible goes on to tell us that when we are *raptured* our bodies will be transformed, never to experience death! We will then begin our new life with Christ and all the believers who died before; their spirits rejoined with their transformed bodies at the same time. Amazing stuff! (Hey…a God who created the universe and everything in it can do this!) Scripture goes on to say we will return to Earth with Jesus at the end of the seven-year reign of the Antichrist to witness Him wiping out this wicked world leader and all that is evil on the Earth. This event will take place in Israel in an area called 'Har-Magedon'(Armageddon). It will be an amazing display of the power of Almighty God who is Christ! (Revelation 16:13-16 and 19:17-21).

This then begins what the Bible calls the thousand years of peace, AKA the Millennium. We, the transformed ones, will be given various positions of service during this time so that all is accomplished according to the will of God. Scripture says the Earth will become like God intended in the Garden of Eden. As I mentioned earlier, there will be some 'new' believers who somehow survive the seven years of God's wrath, and they will be part of the Millennium and eventually have children who will live to be *as old as trees* (Isaiah 65: 22)! There will be no sickness or suffering. The eco system will be restored, so no pollution or damage will happen. No one will be poor or in any need at all!

Even the animal kingdom will be docile, not killing each other! Wow… what are the possibilities? Will we not be eating meat anymore? Could we have any animal for a pet? Hard to even wrap your mind around this, but the Bible hasn't lied about anything yet, so I'm pretty excited to experience this future! An interesting development does occur after several hundred years, however. The people born during this time still have a human 'sin nature' and the free will to act on it. Scripture says Satan has been held back from influencing them, but God will allow him to be free long enough to test those who may need to prove they have chosen Christ and therefore desire to be part of the eternal 'New Heaven and New Earth' to come.

The most important thing to know about our Heavenly Father is that He only wants those who freely *choose* to be with him in His Eternal Kingdom. (Who wants anyone around them who is only there because they have no choice in the first place?)

At the end of the thousand years, Christ will end the power of Satan and his demons (fallen angels)! *They will be 'thrown into the Lake of Fire to be tormented for eternity, never to be released'* (Revelation 20: 7-10 paraphrased).

There are many resources that are available to help in absorbing all this, thankfully; as I am not prepared to include, or explain all that the Bible contains on this subject!

Claire's Dream:

Several years ago, Claire wanted to tell me she had a dream that upset her. She said that in this dream she was raptured and it was wonderful, but it made her very sad because she was all alone! I assured her that dreams were often weird, and we talked more about what the scriptures say concerning this coming event. She never said anything more about the dream and life went on.

We had decided earlier that year to plan a short vacation before the end of summer. Claire had been dealing with various health issues, but we had reserved a cabin near the shore on Puget Sound to spend a few days. Unfortunately, during that stay, things 'went south' when she fell and twisted her knee while climbing a steep slope up from the water where she had been kayaking. After we came home, she said she was not feeling well and was going to drive herself to the hospital to have her knee looked at. She told me she would hopefully be home in a few hours (but it usually took much longer with her State-funded medical care).

She called me about three hours later to say they were keeping her! I was shocked and asked why! She said her blood-draw came back cancerous. My heart took a sudden leap up to my throat, and Claire could tell how upset I was. She kept telling me she had faith that she could be healed and she was ready to deal with whatever was needed.

About a month later, if this news was not enough to deal with, Claire received a letter apologizing for a delayed report. It seems another health provider at a clinic she had been seen at failed to inform her that she had a 'life-threatening blood disorder' that she needed to get checked out! (I later was 'assured' by the oncologists at the hospital that knowing about it sooner would not have made any difference.) *Really?*

We then began a series of despair and hope, remission and infections, treatments and prayer. After almost a year of this, Claire's latest state of remission was invaded by an infection that brought the cancer back full force. I stayed in denial, but Sasha begged to stop Claire's suffering and 'let her go'. Eventually and reluctantly, I resigned myself to a reality I never thought I would face. Despite the best medical efforts, Claire's positive attitude and so many prayers, she took her last earthly breath in the hospital while I kept my hand on her arm, still hoping for a miracle.

The grief of losing your only child (or any child) is hard to describe. I did not know how crushing this kind of grief could be until then. I also know how devastating it was for Sasha to lose her mom at such a young age. It was all so unfair. It should have been me in that hospital bed…I was old, she had a young daughter to raise still! Claire had also become my best friend and helper. She had not been able to keep any job after they saw her misdemeanor record.

Even Goodwill would not give her a chance. (They could have if she had been a felon…a government policy!) I gave her a small 'salary' to be my house-keeper, grocery shopper, gas-the-car and take-it-for-service person, do the laundry and of course be Sasha's mom! (I got spoiled.) She was always fun to talk with and we often cracked each other up over so many silly things!

Like anyone else experiencing the death of a child, I tried my best to accept and understand why God would take her back home before me!

This is such a consuming kind of grief! Several difficult weeks passed before I decided to call a close cousin who had lost her 90-year-old mom earlier. She was very understanding and assured me that the worst waves of grief would come and go, eventually subsiding in their intensity over time. She even sent me a book by C. S. Lewis titled *A Grief Observed*, written after the loss of his beloved wife. (I can attest now that family members who care are a God-send during a time like this.)

At some point I also allowed myself to read through Claire's journal. It was full of ordinary daily musings, like events with Sasha, shopping with me and putting up with my normal complaining about prices, etc. Eventually I came upon the page where she had written about her upsetting 'rapture dream'. She dated every journal entry, and it was jolting when I saw the date on this entry was almost one year before she died.

Throughout scripture God often 'speaks' to people in dreams. My grand-mother died ten years before my grandfather, and he told me about a dream he had about her not long after she passed. He said she looked so young, in-teracting with a group of children playing in a beautiful park-like setting. He believed it was a vision from God meant to assure him she was happy in her eternal life. I now also believe God wanted to prepare Claire and let her know she would be part of His kingdom. I am blessed knowing where she is now, and that someday I can spend as much time with her as she wants to in that amazing, eternal adventure!

Good News/Bad News:

Well, of course, the good news is *LIFE IS ETERNAL!* Sadly, this will be bad news for many! Being a news-junkie now, I spend time with the comment sec-tions of Fox and other sources where I am always amazed by how many people state they don't believe there is anything after we die…or that it will just be endless sleep! Then there are those who claim if someone kills themselves that at least they are out of their pain and 'at peace', believing that death ends everything! Wow…what a sad and hopeless way to live…and I will never understand gambling against God's word concerning eternity.

In addition…what unbelievable arrogance for anyone to basically proclaim that they are 'all-knowing' about this! Actually, they sound a lot like Lucifer, the angel who became Satan, when he announced he would *be like the Most High*' (Isaiah 14:14). It is important to note that scripture also assures us that Satan is *not* equal to God. He is not omnipotent (all powerful), he is not omnipresent (everywhere at once) or omniscient (knowing all things). He cannot create anything and his 'powers' are only what God allows him to have…for now. He does have angelic abilities, and his minions (now demons) who chose to rebel with him can cause a lot of grief in this life until their time is up.

I am no different than any other human when it comes to the many questions I have for Christ when I meet Him! I am still unclear on the topic of predestination and other doctrines that most Christians seem to easily accept! I am not yet able to wrap my mind around the purpose of the unbearable cruelty of the crucifixion, or the mystery of a triune God…but I *know* the resurrection is proof that death is *not* the end of life, and the ultimate proof that Jesus is who He said He was! There is much I need to understand, but I know our human minds are finite and limited in many ways…we are not God, and in fact in Genesis the scripture says we were created a *'little lower than the angels'*…and *they* are not all-knowing either!

The Bible does say that *'now we see through a glass darkly'* (1 Corinthians 13: 12) *'but then when face to face our knowledge will be complete'* (paraphrased). This scripture was written at a time when mirrors, called looking glasses, were a piece of polished brass or silver, offering only a dim reflection. I am in awe of what a time of glorious revelation awaits us!

Even more good news is another amazing message in God's word (IMHO). It claims *when we see Christ we will be* like Him! (1 John 3: 2) SERIOUSLY? Wait…whoa, I mean we can walk on water or into a room without needing to go through a door? What else will we be able to do? My head spins trying to even contemplate all that might lie ahead!

Eternal life is the best possible news as far as I'm concerned! I remember, as a very young child, wondering if this earthly life was all there is. I didn't like that idea at all! Funerals were upsetting, no matter how old the person was, and usually they had suffered for the last years of their life! I thought how unfair it was that even 80 or 90 years was not enough time to experience what this world had to offer! Very wealthy people could experience far more than the average person because they had the income to allow for it!

Then there was the other issue of not having enough time to explore different occupations, ambitions or dreams! I wanted to be an actress…but my life circumstances forced me to be practical in order to support myself. I imagine (and hope) these dreams and longings might be part of what is fulfilled during God's amazing gift of eternal life, and I thank Him every day for this possibility! Yes, it is good news that life is eternal, but bad news for the 'many' Jesus said would choose the *'broad road and wide gate that leads to destruction'* instead of the *'narrow path and small gate'* His believers would choose (Matthew 7: 13-14, paraphrased).

The people on the broad road are those who joke about God being the 'Sky Fairy', or claim Jesus was a liar, or silliest of all, a mythological figure that never existed! They gamble that they are right, and I believe this sad reality is why *Jesus wept over Jerusalem* (Luke 19: 41). Jesus knows eternal suffering awaits those who reject Him, as this is the rejection of *'The Way, the Truth and the Life'*.

How devastating for those who believe their suffering will end if they die! I am not convinced that scripture teaches all suicides will end in eternal suffering, but it does teach that God's justice is perfect, and no one will receive any justice that they do not deserve. (I admit this subject is mind-bending to contemplate!) I do believe that any person who purposely dies taking others with them, or takes their life hoping to hurt or punish another will face the eternal judgment they likely denied was a possibility while alive.

God is love. God is immensely patient and forgiving…but He is also a God of perfect justice who cannot ignore the consequences of unrepentant sin. *He is not willing that* any *should 'perish' (endure endless suffering), but only those who are humble and sincere in their repentance, who love, respect and trust Him will be welcome* (2nd Peter 3:9 paraphrased).

Again, I am astounded at the mindset of an atheist! The amazing creation of God is more than enough to convince me of His majesty, power and truth! Every time I take a minute to notice the incredible design of a butterfly I am overwhelmed by the artistry! In fact, there has never been an artist capable of any original design, photograph or painting that can compete with God's creativity. He is the ultimate artist! Anyone who is not amazed and grateful for the variety of plants and animals alone, or does not recognize the genius of creation is someone I could *never* be friends with!

I remember lying in a tall grassy patch in the back area of my grandparent's property when I was about 5 years old. I was looking closely at a weed I had pulled up. It looked a little like a skinny wheat stalk, with a perfectly woven head on it. The intricate design made me wonder who or what designed it! I am an amateur artist myself and maybe watching my mother draw and paint her fashion designs helped me notice things like this. I see so much in nature to be amazed by, and I know how limited our human efforts are to replicate the majesty and beauty of creation. I simply do not understand atheism at all.

More evidence of 'intelligent design' is the fact that it takes more than twelve years of medical school and years of internship and experience for a doctor to understand even the basics of how our bodies are designed! Even after that they need to select a specified area of medical treatment in order to know just one area of the body well! The discovery of DNA alone should have dispelled any doubt about divine creation! These are just some of the factors that have convinced many scientists that life is not just an accident of evolution. This is why former atheists and agnostics like C.S. Lewis and Albert Einstein came to the conclusion that humans and all of nature must have been created by a divine, intelligent being we call God.

I do believe this is a time of choosing unlike any era in our history! I find myself praying constantly that there is some time left for an 'awakening', because scripture does say that God declares *'if a nation would turn to Him and repent, He will heal their land!'* (Jeremiah 18:8 and 2 Chronicles 7: 14-15 paraphrased).

He does keep His promises…and *that* would be incredible to witness, and it just might happen if enough of us turn to Him!

(75) ~ Friday ~ July ~ 18TH: ~ 2014 ~
(Before her cancer diagnosis)
~ A Nice cool Down in The Temps..!
~ Reeeally sunburned from yester-
Day @ The River. ~ Didn't do a whole
LoT Today ~ Due To The OUCH + Dis-
comfort of The SunBurn. A.J. +
Frog kept me company This afternoon.
~ Dropped them off @ A.J.'s ~ Later.
~ STARTING A New Book; 'Heaven Changes
Everything' = So Good ~ So fAR! :)
✗ ~ HAD A really weird DREAM last Night.
~ I WAS RApTUReD = WHICH WAS cool!
~ BuT everybody I love on earth ~
wasn't with me! ‼ ~ Dreams Are
So Freakin' weird?!!? ~ ~
~ Got A little Gossip from The neighbor-
Hood ~ Break-ups + WHAT NOT? ~
~ Jesus ~ Come quickly ~ because
This world is A Trip !?.! :)

Claire's Dream

Chapter 16
OUR BLESSED HOPE

When it is my time, and I see my grandfather, I will let him know how prophetic he was about his comments regarding the trends he saw and shared with me that day in 1963. I will also thank him and my grandmother for being the Godly influence in my life!

Now in the year 2023, it is hard to believe the incredible evil happening everywhere we look! I cannot help but believe that the prophecies of what the scriptures call the 'end times' is taking place. Bible scholars say we are to look at Israel as God's timetable, as all prophecy is related to His plan for the redemption of His 'chosen', and this includes Gentiles (all non-Jews who believe in Him). I greatly respect the perspective on all this by a ministry called 'Olive Tree Ministries', a Messianic 'church' started by Jewish people who came to accept Jesus as the prophesized Messiah. I started listening to them after 9-11 because they intersperse the Judeo-Christian Bible truth with what is going on in the news. I appreciate how they end most of their programs with declaring that 'Prophecy was not meant to scare us, but to prepare us!'

I also believe that all of us alive now need to be brave enough to speak out against all the wrong we see when we see it! Children are being told that they can be the opposite sex if they 'feel like it'! Our own president, Joe Biden, and the Democrat Party support medically altering children to achieve this diabolical idea! Laws are being ignored, crime is being tolerated and everything the '60s bullet hit is exacerbating daily! So much is backwards; words are losing their true meanings; women and men, including our Democrats in government, are supporting the abortion of babies even up to their birth! We are seeing George Orwell's disturbing novel, *1984*, coming true with our own government creating the destructive policies described there!

One of the most frightening scriptures concerning God's judgments is found in Romans 1: 24-32. *"Therefore God gave them over in the sinful desires of their hearts to sexual impurity for the degrading of their bodies with one another."* These verses go on to describe same-sex relations, and includes all the unnatural perversions we see these days. It then states that *any who approve of, or cele-*

brate, these things are equally condemned! It is the 'gave them over' part that makes me cringe, because it could mean their fate is sealed! I pray that all who love righteousness understand that silence is also consent, and our elections truly do have consequences!

Despite all this, I believe the God I have come to love wants us to be 'Happy Warriors' (a phrase used by President Regan whenever he talked about fighting for freedom and righteousness here in America). We do not know the date or time and may have decades or more before God's judgment and the 'rapture' promised by Christ! We need to be the 'salt and light' that helps bring hope and peace of mind to anyone open to learning about it. We can do that by being happy warriors!

My grandparents were serious people, but never unhappy! They were content with their life, gentle and respectful with everyone they interacted with. I am looking forward to seeing them again. I will be anxious to know if my grandfather has spent any time with his beloved Abraham Lincoln! I want to see what my grandmother has been doing…and I'm pretty sure it will not be darning socks or slaving over a hot stove, canning produce she grew herself! Most of all I am filled with happy anticipation, knowing that they will also be with me when we return with Christ at the end of the Tribulation (His second coming) to begin the promised Millennium!

An Incredible Future:

This promise is almost too unreal to speculate about, let alone imagine…but before eternity we will have that 1000-year period called the Millennium! It is the reason for the 'blessed hope' after the Rapture when we return with him at the end of the seven years to restore the Earth! There is a lot we can visualize about this, but I am just inspired and hopeful, thinking about all that is possible! I know that God's word assures each of us that we have certain gifts, talents and abilities that will be used and perfected during that time!

I think about my neighbor who is currently a New-Ager, but could be put in charge of Earth's new Department of Agriculture…directing the growing of all the produce needed, if she just accepts Christ! (She also raises chickens along with her incredible gardens!) This Millennium Kingdom will use every ability of every believer! We will not be bored, but trusted to accomplish all that is needed in maintaining this earthly paradise. I believe there will be athletic competition, music and performance entertainment as well! (I have been told by some that I could have been an actress as well as a stand-up comedian…so?)

My granddaughter, Sasha, has a great sense of decor and artistic talent, with a strong work ethic and fun personality that God will happily use as well! She tells me often that one of her hopes in the afterlife is to be smothered with kittens! (LOL, I actually can relate, and I bet we can experience that as well). Sometimes I lay awake happy, just visualizing all the possibilities that await us! Jesus said He was preparing a home for each of us as well! *'In my Father's house are many mansions. I go there now to prepare a place for you. If it were not so I would have told you…'* (Paraphrased from John 14: 2-6).

We will certainly not be resting on a cloud, harp in hand, but experiencing all that is mentioned here as well as the most satisfying, glorious worship of God that just defies speculation!

I am overwhelmed trying to visualize it all!

Happy Warriors Needed:

It is easy to be consumed by the evil we are bombarded with every day unless we are living in a cave somewhere with no way to know what is going on! But God's word suggests that He needs us to be 'Happy Warriors' in order to battle not only with human evil but against the *'Powers and Principalities, against spiritual wickedness in high places'*! (Ephesians 6: 12). This spiritual battle will be won by Jesus and all His believers! His Word tells us how it ends; therefore, we can help others to understand the amazing happiness and full life they could share in this world as well as in God's eternal kingdom just by accepting the promise and grace of His forgiveness!

I am beginning to believe we need to focus more on this indescribable future promised for us by Christ and written about in scripture! There is an old saying about catching more flies with honey or something…so maybe besides being truthful about God's judgments we need to include the promise of this eternal happiness with equal fervor!

I remember a conversation with Claire about being a Christian when she was in-between her 'street life' phase. She told me about two church-going ladies she talked with about God and Heaven. Apparently they knew Claire smoked cigarettes and liked to party, so they laughed when she told them she hoped there was 'some level' of Heaven she might be allowed into when she died. They claimed to be Christian, but firmly proclaimed that God would *never* allow someone like her into His kingdom!

This, unfortunately, is how people are misled, discouraged and even turned away from God's truth and redeeming love. I thank God that Claire was open to hear my assurance that these ladies were what Jesus would call 'all for show', having a *'form of godliness but denying its power'* (2nd Timothy 3:5 paraphrased). Claire fully accepted Christ shortly after that, and before she passed, she shared her new faith humbly and happily with anyone who wanted to know her story.

Lighten-up Francis:

I really have a hard time with Bible-thumpers like the two 'church ladies'. There are too many Christians who insult and look down on those who do not share their version of Jesus! I have talked to some who have a friend or relative that is a 'seeker', and they only tell them how wrong they are while threatening them with Hellfire! Well, God LOVES a seeker! I wish these folks would just remind them of Christ's promise that if we SEEK, we shall FIND! Anyone who truly is seeking the truth of God will eventually be shown it! There are many authenticated stories of countless seekers who had almost unexplainable experiences that brought them to faith in the true God. I read about one who actually found a Bible, translated into his own language, on the ground when he tripped on it! (Google is a friend for anyone interested in this subject.)

Another example is the history of a wonderful Messianic Congregation called Beit Tikvah (House of Hope in Hebrew). It was founded, and currently headed by a Jewish couple, Hylan and Rita Slobokin. They freely share their journey of seeking true faith for years, traveling the world and sitting at the feet of religious leaders in India and elsewhere. This was in the '70s when the New-Age movement was captivating so many of that generation. Hylan and Rita were looking for more than what their family and religious traditions were offering, but despite their search they were not finding the satisfaction they were longing for.

In telling their story, they are convinced that God intervened when they eventually encountered a group of fellow 'seekers' that turned out to be in a kind of Christian commune. They stayed long enough to learn the 'truth' that

Jesus said would 'set them free'. The rest of the story is the happiness and knowledge they share with so many lucky enough to attend their services. Sasha and I attended only one time, and if it wasn't such a long drive, we would be there every Saturday! (Messianic services are on Saturdays, called the Shabbat, just as Jewish services are.)

Jesus said that *'No one comes to Me unless the Father has sent them'* (John 6:44 paraphrased). Seeking God the Father is the first step, but to reject the Son is to reject the Father! This is how God knows we believe in Him after the sacrifice and resurrection of Christ. (If pointing this out to a 'seeker' is not accepted, I would just send up a prayer that a seed was planted and move on.) Jesus never argued, He just stated His truth.

Chapter 17
TRUTH MATTERS

An unfortunate issue now is the growing number of churches that are going 'woke' and only teach what they think is non-offensive culturally. Their reasoning seems to be a fear of losing attendees, or being called bigoted if they were to teach the actual truth of God that offends many! Because of this thinking, most churches today completely ignore the book of Revelation and the prophecies of God's coming judgments. I have recently been informed that most Bible Seminaries no longer teach their students about this most important last book of the Bible! This is a very unfortunate path to take as God's word says those who read it will be blessed.

Jesus (Yeshua in Hebrew) said that *'many would stray from the faith in the last days'* (1ˢᵗ Timothy, 4: 1) Claire and I left a church like that, and I now attend a small Messianic Congregation that is closer to where I live than the one I mentioned earlier. I prefer the whole truth of God's messages in the Old as well as the New Testament. I also love learning how the Jewish Torah relates to everyday life, as well as how prophesy is proven by historical facts and is actually explaining some current world events! (This is hard to find in many traditional Christian churches.)

The most important point about sharing Christian beliefs is that browbeating, or demeaning a non-believer will never win anyone over. I do wish I had known what I know now when I was visited by Jehovah Witnesses and the Mormon 'missionaries' who came by! I have read the Book of Mormon and the Jehovah Witness Bible, so I am ready if the occasion arises again! Mormons teach that Jesus is a 'brother of Satan' (aka Lucifer) and therefore only an angel! Since they claim the Book of Mormon is 'just another gospel of Christ', I would simply point out that the much older, original Biblical Gospel states that *Jesus actually created the angels and He is above all creation and part of the Holy Trinity of God!* (Colossians 1:16 paraphrased). I would just ask them to do a little more study of that first Gospel so they can maybe ask their fellow members about that. (The problem is that they, like the Jehovah Witnesses, are not allowed to read anything but their own texts.) Suggesting this idea to them might not help…but slamming the door in their faces is also not helpful! These people are good-hearted and deserve to hear the truth in a compassionate way! There are *many* other Mormon and Jehovah Witness teachings that can be countered, teachings that lead to a lot of odd concepts and hypocrisy, but that would take several more pages for me to cover here! (There are several books on this subject if one is interested.) One important fact is that, unlike the Christian Bible, there is no historical evidence that backs up any of the places or people the Book of Mormon describes, just as there are no justifications for the altered scriptures in the JW version of the Bible that can mislead a seeker!

If or when I have the opportunity to speak with one, I will challenge the claim that their Bible is the same as the Christian Bible. The following from any standard Christian Bible is found in John 1:1, *"In the beginning was the Word. And the Word was with God and the Word was God."* And in 1:14, *"The Word became flesh and dwelt among men."* The 'Word' is Jesus, but in the Jehovah Witness Bible (called The New World Translation), it states, "and the Word was a god: (with a small g)! They claim their Bible uses the same scriptures, but that is a lie. In all of their *Watchtower* magazines, they only describe Christ as 'The greatest man who ever lived.' They deny His deity, just as the Mormons, Muslims, Hindus, Buddhists and New-Agers, etc. do!

True Freedom:

Jesus said, *"If you continue in My word you are truly My disciples and you will know the truth and the truth will set you free"* (John 8:31- 32).

Without knowing who God really is and what He really wants for us is critical! Without the truth we can fall for any cult or false teaching and find nothing but confusion, hypocrisy and unhappiness in this world (let alone the next)! For example, I am thinking of the time I went to my older brother's home for a family Christmas dinner and gift exchange. One of his wife's sisters was there who had recently become a Jehovah Witness. When it came time to open the gifts, she had to excuse herself and stayed in another room until we were done because her religion does not allow members to participate in this holiday tradition! This same restriction applies to birthdays and Easter, even for children. (Apparently they are unaware that Jesus celebrated every Jewish holiday and traditional occasions with His fellow Jews!) These beliefs have to be especially hard on the JW children! At a public school they are not allowed to say the Pledge of Allegiance, putting their hands over their hearts. This, on top of no holidays or other class celebrations, cannot make for a very happy childhood.

Another misunderstood belief, even among some Christians, is that we should always separate religion from politics. This is where I would point out that Jesus had plenty to say about the 'politics' of His day. The root word of politics is from the Greek word 'politika' and 'polis' for city. *Affairs of The City* is a book about politics by Aristotle. (In other words, politics are about people and how they live.)

The difference is that in Jesus' day there was no such thing as democracy like we have today! No leaders were elected by the people! In fact, I might be mistaken, but I don't think there were any 'elected' government positions until after Christianity took hold. Jesus instructed that all people should respect their 'governments' but honor the things of God. He often spoke against the leaders of His day as being hypocrites and unjust, but He specifically targeted the religious 'leaders' who were dictating public affairs.

God actually created and ordained government, in order to oversee the safety and protection, as well as the laws and justice in each nation! But throughout early history all nations were subject to Kings or dictators, and the commoner's opinions did not matter. As far as the separation of church and state, America's Constitution only says the government cannot mandate a specific sect of *Christianity*, like Lutheran, Baptist or Catholic, etc! The founders wanted to make sure Americans had the freedom to choose. They did not want a government sanctioned Church of America like they had with the Church of England! The so-called 'separation of church and state' found in Jefferson's writings is used by unbelievers to justify their anti-Christian political policies. We have freedom *of* religion, not freedom *from* religion! Any trip to Washington, DC that includes a tour of the historical sites and monuments will make it very clear that this nation was founded on Christianity. Even our currency has 'In God We Trust' engraved on our money since the first dollar was printed!

We are so blessed to live in a nation founded on godly principals, so I am annoyed beyond belief at any American citizen who does not vote! I will boldly declare to their faces that not voting *is* voting…voting for the status quo! This is *not* acceptable, especially if you claim to be a Christian! In the mid-term election of 2022, there was so much that needed to change if America was to heal from all the social and economic damage that has occurred just in the past two years under a president that ignores almost every Christian teaching, including the right to life for the unborn!

We had massive damage from the Chinese virus (COVID 19) 'pandemic' with horrific over-reactions, senseless mandates and job losses! Children missed two years of education due to the classes only being offered online! In addition, we are also seeing lawlessness and immorality that are almost biblical in their intensity, boldness and frequency! Our police are defunded and restrained while criminals are released to repeat their demonic activity with little or no consequences!

These are government policy issues! Our natural energy sources are being restricted and even vowed to be destroyed by the current POTUS, Joe Biden! This is creating unprecedented issues world-wide! The economy is failing for all but the very wealthy! Our food supply is threatened by the huge cost increases to the farmers for fertilizer, fuel, equipment and transportation! Our children are being taught that they can change their gender; and our political leaders, including healthcare agencies, are allowing this! These are all things our POTUS and elected representatives are paid to monitor and correct if needed!

God's word has a lot to say about governments and their leaders not acting as God wills. Proverbs 29:2 says, *"When the righteous increase the people rejoice, But when a wicked man rules people groan."* And in verse 12 it states, *"If a Ruler pays attention to falsehood all his ministers become wicked."* (This has never been more evident here in America than it is now!)

Scripture also asks believers to pray for our leaders; 1st Timothy 2:1-2 says, *"First of all, then, I urge that entreaties and prayers, petitions and thanksgivings, be made on behalf of all men, for Kings and all who are in authority, so that we may lead a tranquil and quiet life in all godliness and dignity."* Then 2nd Chronicles 7:14 (regarding a possible judgment) says, *"...and My people who are called by My name humble themselves and pray and seek My face and turn from their wicked ways, then I will hear from heaven, will forgive their sin and will heal their land."* These are just two of many verses that verify God's will for us to pray for all who rule over us!

Jesus often spoke about truth, even declaring that 'He WAS the truth' (John 14: 6). I have lately thought about how important it is to know what is true about Jesus. One thing that came to me was how I would feel if people believed I was not the person I am! For instance, if someone believed, and even told others, that I was a skilled mechanic or an Olympic swimmer I would not appreciate it! Even worse if they believed I had molested a child or robbed a bank! The point is that getting it wrong about me would make me *very* upset, but getting it wrong about God has an *eternal* consequence!

Chapter 18
BULLET PROOF

Was the '60s bullet 'a shot heard around the world'? I'm thinking yes, because it seems the damage to society is evident in every 'civilized' country now! It is more difficult to assess because our media focuses on this country, and the problems are overwhelming today! My grandfather's fear that folks were 'beginning to confuse liberty with license' has proven to be warranted.

If you have young children, you are now faced with the reality that they are no longer safe from the push to question the gender they were born with! Even our elected representatives are bowing to this evil agenda! Public school teachers are adding this to their curriculum starting in kindergarten! In addition, we are witnessing the devaluing and defunding of our law enforcement, and the growing number of judges and district attorneys who will not enforce the laws as written are forcing many to buy guns for their families protection and self defense!

Drugs like fentanyl are now even unknowingly or deceptively dispersed and killing thousands…a disaster and legacy of the '60s mantra to get high! And no one seems to be asking why so many are willing to risk their lives to be in an altered state of mind! This drug, often used with meth, is said to also cause such severe psychosis that the users cannot function normally, are extremely violent and living on the streets of every major city. Our open southern border is allowing this scourge as well as human trafficking, rape and child abuse at a level never seen before!

Christians are under attack on many levels now, called bigots and racists if expressing their pro-life or pro-law values! We are called un-loving and intolerant if we even offer the opinion that children should not be told they can change their gender, or if we dare suggest that the 'trans' movement is a destructive, science-denying *fad* (which it is)! Anti-Semitism is ramping up as well, and Israel is constantly being threatened! Immorality and same-sex relations are not just tolerated but *celebrated*! The LGBTQ+ community has just added 'Minor-Attracted' (people who prefer sex with kids under 18) to their growing list of sexual identities!

As stated before in this book, it is hard to deny that this looks an awful lot like what is described in scripture as the signs of the 'end times' when Christ will come for His own! We are warned to be prepared: *"For our struggle is not against flesh and blood, but against the rulers, against the authorities, against the powers of this dark world and against the spiritual forces of evil in the heavenly realms"* (Ephesians 6: 12 NIV).

So how do we become 'bullet proof'? Well, in that same letter to the church in Ephesus in verse 11, Paul the Apostle writes that we must *"Put on the full armor of God that you may be able to stand against the Devil's schemes."*

There is much more written in Paul's extensive description of the 'armor of God', but most believers (including me) interpret it as his emphasis on how necessary this protection will be, *knowing* who the enemy is and how difficult the battle will be. But it is vital to understand that this 'armor' can only protect if we truly *know* God for who He is!

Who Is God?

'Not everyone who says to me Lord, Lord will enter the Kingdom of heaven. On that day many will say: did we not do many great things in your name, prophesying, healing, etc...? Then I will tell them plainly, I never knew you...depart from me you workers of lawlessness.' (Matthew 7: 21-23 paraphrased.) As far as I'm concerned, this response from Christ would end my world...even imagining it now sends a feeling of dread I would never want to experience standing before Him!

Jesus referred to himself by many different 'titles': *the Bread of Life* (John 6:35), *Son of Man* (Luke 19:10), *the Alpha and the Omega* (Revelation 22:13), *the Good Shepherd* (John 10:11), the *Light of the World* (John 8:12), the *Resurrection and the Life* (John 11:25), and many more if you care to research with our friend Google! Scripture actually records about 200 names and titles to describe Him! Jesus also flat-out declared Himself *to be* the prophesized *Messiah* when he encountered the Samaritan woman at the well, found in John 4:1-42.

Knowing who God is, the trinity of Father, Son and Holy Spirit, is a matter of eternal life! The only way to know this truth is by learning what Holy Scripture says about this Holy Trinity. The sad state of too many churches today is that they are not teaching the whole truth or are giving a distorted view of it! It is up to each of us to be more willing to seek it from scripture, as well as from those who have studied it carefully and prayerfully. I have learned that if any writings or 'sermons' sound suspect, it is best to verify what is said by finding out if the Bible actually supports it!

The importance of knowing the truth about Christ cannot be stressed enough! If Jesus should tell any of us to 'depart from Him because He never knew us'…it will be because *we* never knew *Him*! He is who He said He was! Before His crucifixion He also told His followers that He would send His Holy Spirit to comfort and help them after He was gone, ascended into Heaven. Who is the Holy Spirit? He is the Spirit of Truth! In John 16: 13-15, Jesus says, *"But when He, the Spirit of truth comes, He will guide you into all the truth; for He will not speak on His own initiative, but whatever He hears, He will speak; and He will disclose to you what is to come. He will glorify me, for He will take of Mine and will disclose it to you. All things that the Father has are Mine; therefore I said that He takes of Mine and will disclose it to you."*

This is powerful information, and I wish more churches would expound on this subject! How incredible and wonderful is this?

If ever there was a time to decide, I believe it is now! I do not believe God wants us to just 'hunker down' and wait for Christ to appear. If we trust in Him, we are free to live without fear knowing who wins in the end! We are to be watchful and helpful, using every opportunity to speak His truth, thankful for each day! Jesus called this the purpose and blessing of being *'In the world…but not of the world'* (John 17: 14-15 paraphrased). This simply means we are to understand that this world we live in now is not all there is, and God wants us to be 'Holy' as He is 'Holy'. The word holy actually translates as separate or set apart…not living or acting like many who reject God or believe our *liberty* gives us the *license* to indulge in whatever the world finds desirable. At the same time, we are not expected to live like perfect saints; or become like the Mennonites, Amish and others who restrict their followers in ways Jesus would not!

My grandparents eventually realized that while the Mennonite restrictions were definitely not *'of the world'*; this church misunderstood Christ's teaching by neglecting the *'in the world'* part! (I am grateful for their realization and decision to leave that church!) The Mennonites and many other restrictive churches, also described as *legalistic*, are guilty of this and it results in hypocrisy and unhappiness! The Jehovah Witness beliefs about Christ, politics and salvation-by-works are not supported by the scriptures they claim to follow. These unbiblical teachings do not draw anyone closer to God or help them cope with life's difficulties! They only distort the truth, condemning many to eternal darkness.

These beliefs have also resulted in abusive practices that have surfaced within these quasi-Christian religious sects, and as true believers we need to speak the truth out of *love* to anyone who needs to hear it! Explaining how these beliefs are not supported in scripture, without any berating or condemnation, can be helpful…there is no need to be an obnoxious, condemning *Bible-thumper*!

With Christ we have the *freedom* to be our best selves, even with our imperfect ways, knowing we are each a work-in-progress! We are free and blessed to lift up and encourage everyone God puts in our paths and be happy doing it! And best of all, we are *free of the fear of death!* That is *true* liberty!

We have an unbelievable, indescribable and amazing future! Each of us can be sure that we have a great purpose now, no matter our age or situation. God has given us His wisdom to do this through His Holy word and *the* 'Word' (Jesus) *who became flesh and dwelt among us!* We have the blessing of the Holy Spirit to comfort and guide us. We truly do have all we need to be the *Happy Warriors* that will win this battle, and then enjoy what He has promised in our never-ending life with Him!

A recent radio minister I was listening to talked about how much our awesome God wants us to be close to Him. He went on to say we should have no hesitation in 'pestering' Him with the smallest issues we are faced with! In this Pastor's understanding, he believes that God cares deeply about everything each of His followers care about, and He wants to hear all we wish to share… the good, bad and the ugly!

Well, interestingly enough, one of my favorite Bible verses is *'God notices, even when a* Sparrow *falls…'* (Matthew 10: 29-31 paraphrased). That is just part of this passage on how important humans are to Him, as it concludes with the assurance that we are more valuable than *'many sparrows'!*

I am starting to believe this Pastor's view as well! I find myself praying more often as if I'm talking to a friend I trust will care and patiently listen to my many concerns and ramblings! It may seem a little improper or irreverent…but maybe it's not to Him? (I only wish I had known this blessing decades ago!) Again, the words of Jesus come to mind; that knowing the truth would set us free… and that *truth* comes from knowing Him!

Jesus said to lay all our burdens on Him, declaring *'my yoke is light'* (Matthew 11: 28-30 paraphrased). He truly cares and wants us to be close to Him! And when we hear the phrase 'The Passion of the Christ', we need to understand that His 'passion' to offer us an eternal life with Him was so strong that he agreed to take on all the ugly sin of the world (and ours) as He suffered horrendous torture, shedding the only blood that our holy Father would accept as the final sacrifice that would make this possible. This is the sacrifice that tore in half the massive, 45-60-foot high, 4-inch thick curtain that kept worshipers from approaching God! Before Christ's crucifixion and resurrection, an approach was only possible through the High Priest who alone could accept a blood sacrifice and present it to God behind that curtain! This is what Jesus meant when he cried out from the cross, *"It is finished!"* (John 19:30). The supernatural tearing in two of that great curtain was witnessed by many and recorded in scripture (Mark 15: 38).

I do not pretend to comprehend God's reasoning…I can only find comfort in the promise that we will understand clearly in His time. Of course Jesus knew He would be resurrected 'supernaturally', but His suffering as a human was as real as any could be here on Earth. The incredible blessing is *He is alive*, waiting for the Father's permission to return for us!

The Bible is such a massive collection of wisdom, historic events, warnings, truth, promises, timeless illustrations of life and human nature that I feel overwhelmed knowing how little I know! One of my biggest regrets is not getting serious about it before I had lived almost fifty years!

Predestined?

I do believe those of us who are alive at this time are here for a predestined mission (and I do have some questions about the doctrine of predestination, but I will save that for Christ!).

I cannot help but be amazed and wondering why I am alive with these 'end-times' Bible prophecies happening in real time! It cannot be by accident! Everything Jesus told His followers is unfolding daily now! The lawlessness, sexual deviance, wars and rumors of wars, pestilence, crazy weather and natural disasters, children turning against their parents, cold-hearted cruelty…etc.! All occurring with more intensity and frequency like labor pains, just as He said it would be!

My faith in the truth of the Bible mostly comes from the fact that all the prophecy recorded there has proven absolutely accurate so far! There are no inaccuracies in general to be found with any writers of these Holy Scriptures and none by our Lord Jesus…so there is no reason to not believe it will occur as written! *What a gift from God!*

This is a blessing I never expected to see before I died. I marvel at the very possibility that I and many others may actually defy the old adage 'No one gets out of here alive'!

Supernatural:

If all of this sounds supernatural, it's because it *is*! **God** is supernatural, the many miracles recorded and the promise of eternal paradise sounds, and will *be* supernatural! The virgin birth of Jesus (exactly as prophesized), and the claim by His Disciples that there were *too many* miracles to write down is certainly beyond our natural experience! And the 'catching up' of His believers to escape the coming judgment of God will *definitely* be supernatural! Despite how it sounds, I am thinking that these things might be considered supernatural by our earthly standards, but it all sounds just *SUPER* to me!

When I think about the times I was in some real danger, I'm certain I was blessed with some supernatural help from His angels! He had not given up on me, so now I'm more convinced He has a plan that has become more evident as I write. This is why I believe that many who are alive now are here to be part of His end-times plan to rescue as many as possible from the judgments to come!

God's Time Clock:

I must repeat the fact that most Bible scholars agree Israel is God's *time clock* and the focus of His plan for judgment and eternity, fulfilling His promise in prophecy to reveal His grace and provide redemption through Christ. The scriptures also declare that Jerusalem, now the official capital of Israel (thanks to President Trump), would be a *'stumbling block to the nations'*! Throughout history, and still today, Israel faces constant threats and prejudice from all sides. Zechariah 12:3 says in the last days it will be a *'burdensome stone to the world'*! Even more important, Jerusalem will be the city Christ will establish His rule in for the 1000-year millennium! But before the millennium, halfway through the seven-year tribulation, the Antichrist will enter the future rebuilt third temple in Jerusalem, claim to be God and demand to be worshipped! This will usher in the worst of the horrific judgments described in Revelations. Yes indeed, scripture and history reveal that Israel is the *epicenter* of all God's plans.

When Israel became a nation in a *single day* in 1948, it was the fulfillment of prophecies that are almost 3000 years old! (One that was written about 700 years before Christ is found in Isaiah 66: 7-9.)

No nation in history has ever been formed in a single day! God finally gave them their own country just as He promised after over 2000 years scattered around the world, including the centuries of slavery due to their disobedience! This is what some believe the Bible says will be a sign for the generation that will witness the return of Christ! (There is so much written on this one prophecy alone and I am not qualified to expound on it all here.) Scripture says we are to *pray for the peace of Israel* and be mindful of His desire and the prophecy that *'All Israel will be saved'* according to His will. (Romans 11: 25-27). But, with more in-depth study you will understand this does not mean every Hebrew/Jewish *person* is saved!

I am not an expert on this subject, it is just my supposition that God wanted a segment of humanity to become an example of His holiness; setting them apart and 'choosing' the Hebrews for this purpose. This is why, in my opinion, the Old Testament rules and punishments were as harsh for them as described! God also knew they would rebel and would therefore be punished for centuries while giving the Gentiles the opportunity to be *grafted in to the vine* that is Israel. The eventual sacrifice of Jesus, also called *Yeshua* (*'He who saves'* in Hebrew), made this possible!

It is also important to realize that along with all the mystery and blessings of the supernatural, it is not always from God! For instance, as mentioned previously, many believe that UFOs are supernatural 'messengers' from God…neglecting the scriptures that say that fallen angels, called demons, can create deceptive illusions as well as appear as humans and even *angels of light*! The Bible describes the last days as a time when many will perform 'miracles' that will deceive the whole world. It warns that unexplained supernatural events will occur with the Antichrist, such as his amazing military success and the 'deadly wound' he miraculously recovers from! Too much to write about here… but no matter how disturbing it all sounds, those of us who know the truth have no need to fear and every reason to have the *'Peace that passes all understanding'*!

Realities:

The generation that my grandfather said was confusing liberty with license is still with us, making policies and decisions that affect every one of us and all future generations! Our current government is acting like a dictatorship, supporting the godless ideas that our gender can be switched and promoting the 'Critical Race Theory' that all Caucasian people are born racist and must be punished! Along with these lies they are also dismissive of the plausible conclusion (IMHO) that the Creator of this planet actually *designed* the climate to change! Instead they continue to claim that we humans can control or destroy it! These evil, false beliefs are causing children and many adults horrific anxiety, even resulting in a growing number of child suicides!

Our leaders are also refusing to enforce the laws needed to keep us safe and are even forcing the military to focus on 'preferred pronouns' for transsexual acceptance instead of training our brave men and women how to kill the enemy and break stuff when necessary! They also support the murder of unborn babies without restriction, calling abortion *women's health* and using our taxes to pay for it! They refuse to enforce our southern border which is bringing more deadly drugs and the trafficking of women and children, as well as diseases and hardship for our own citizens! In addition, they have forced millions to lose their jobs simply because they made the choice to refuse a questionable 'vaccine' that research is showing to be almost useless and possibly harmful! They are also supporting the same violence we saw in the late '60s and '70s…a replay of domestic terrorism from the Weather Underground, Black Power and Black Panthers now replaced by Black Lives Matter Inc., Antifa and various eco-terror activist organizations! (And they expect us to accept this violence as just 'peaceful protesting' because they believe it is all justified.)

There is corruption at the highest levels due to the love of money as well as the desire to have a *one-world* government! Our current president is bowing to the Communist Chinese dictator and putting America in great danger just to protect his family's wealth and power! (And I am barely scratching the surface of all that is wrong!)

Despite all this truth, there is a bigger truth! These things are but shadows of the wickedness to come. But righteous judgments will also come, and we know from God Himself who wins in the end!

Blessed Are We:

I am in awe of this time we are in! I am amazed at the fact I am alive to witness Bible prophecy being fulfilled! I am so grateful for my grandparents and every lesson, painful or not, that God has graced me with!

Just the blessing of my grandparents leaving Germany to become Americans and my being born and raised in this exceptional country are gifts from God! The blessings of having my own small house, with hot and cold running water…*indoors,* and enough income to have food and clothing of a variety and abundance unknown in many parts of this world humbles me! How anyone can be ungrateful with these blessings is beyond my understanding!

I am so grateful that God never gave up on me, that His Holy Spirit was *included* after accepting Christ… just as He promised (And I have only recently learned to appreciate *this* gift!). Thanks to finding a small Messianic congregation called *Lion of Judah.* I am receiving more insight into God's truth than I ever learned from most churches. If you are fortunate to attend a true Bible-teaching church, you are indeed blessed!

I am blessed to know I will see my daughter, my immigrant grandparents, and all who have gone before me when it is my time! I was also blessed by the friend who introduced me to Christ in junior high! All these things, even the *timing* of my birth, allowed me to avoid a direct hit from that '60s bullet!

I believe there is a reason for everything and am amazed that I am witnessing so much happening so quickly! I am blessed because I might still have the opportunity to help others see what I am seeing. Maybe they will want to seek the truth that will bless them as well! This is my hope, that my life, whatever is left of it, can be spent encouraging and assuring as many as possible that the plans God has for all who love Him will be more wonderful, spectacular and fulfilling than anything we could possibly imagine!

"For I know the plans I have for you, declares the Lord, plans to prosper you and not to harm you, plans to give you hope and a future. Then you will call on me and come and pray to me and I will listen to you. You will seek me and find me when you seek me with all your heart."

(Jeremiah 29: 11-13) NIV

Acknowledgements

As a first-time author, I would like to acknowledge the support from those who encouraged me to pursue writing this book, especially the input I received from my granddaughter, Alexxa Hendershott! Acting as my pseudo 'editor' and advisor, she provided some needed perspective from her much younger generational viewpoint.

Last, but not least, I want to thank the professional staff at Dorrance Publishing for their skills and caring attention that made this endeavor a rewarding reality for me.